TIME
ANNUAL
1999-2000

TIME
ANNUAL

TOM ABLE-GREEN—ALLSPORT

1999-2000

By the Editors of TIME

TIME ANNUAL 1999-2000

120

66

44

FABRICE COFFRINI—KEYSTONE–AP/WIDE WORLD (BALLOON); BROOKS KRAFT—CORBIS SYGMA FOR TIME (BRADLEY);
ANDREW SULLIVAN—AP (GORE); TAKA FOR TIME DIGITAL (VIDEOGAME); ILLUSTRATION FOR TIME BY ISMAEL ROLDAN (YELTSIN);
ELSA—ALLSPORT (HAMM); SION TOUHIG—CORBIS SYGMA (ECLIPSE); UPI—CORBIS BETTMANN (KENNEDY)

THE YEAR IN REVIEW

88

114

104

156

TIME ANNUAL 1999-2000

MANAGING EDITOR	Kelly Knauer
ART DIRECTOR	Ellen Fanning
PICTURE EDITOR	Patricia Cadley
RESEARCH DIRECTOR	Kathleen Brady
PRODUCTION EDITOR	Michael Skinner
COPY EDITORS	Bruce Christopher Carr (chief), Bob Braine
PRODUCTION DIRECTOR	John Calvano
TIME SPECIAL PROJECTS EDITOR	Barrett Seaman

TIME INC. HOME ENTERTAINMENT

PRESIDENT	Stuart Hotchkiss
EXECUTIVE DIRECTOR, BRANDED BUSINESSES	David Arfine
EXECUTIVE DIRECTOR, NON-BRANDED BUSINESSES	Alicia Longobardo
EXECUTIVE DIRECTOR, TIME INC. BRAND LICENSING	Risa Turken
DIRECTOR, MARKETING SERVICES	Michael Barrett
DIRECTOR, RETAIL & SPECIAL SALES	Tom Mifsud
ASSOCIATE DIRECTORS	Roberta Harris, Kenneth Maehlum
PRODUCT MANAGERS	Andre Okolowitz, Niki Viswanathan, Daria Raehse
ASSOCIATE PRODUCT MANAGERS	Dennis Sheehan, Meredith Shelley, Bill Totten, Lauren Zaslansky
ASSISTANT PRODUCT MANAGERS	Victoria Alfonso, Jennifer Dowell, Ann Gillespie
LICENSING MANAGER	JoAnna West
ASSOCIATE LICENSING MANAGER	Regina Feiler
ASSOCIATE MANAGER, RETAIL & NEW MARKETS	Bozena Szwagulinski
EDITORIAL OPERATIONS DIRECTOR	John Calvano
BOOK PRODUCTION MANAGER	Jessica McGrath
ASSISTANT BOOK PRODUCTION MANAGER	Jonathan Polsky
BOOK PRODUCTION COORDINATOR	Kristen Lizzi
FULFILLMENT DIRECTOR	Richard Perez
ASSISTANT FULFILLMENT MANAGER	Tara Schimming
FINANCIAL DIRECTOR	Tricia Griffin
FINANCIAL MANAGER	Robert Dente
ASSOCIATE FINANCIAL MANAGER	Steven Sandonato
EXECUTIVE ASSISTANT	Mary Jane Rigoroso

THE WRITING OF THE FOLLOWING TIME STAFF MEMBERS AND CONTRIBUTORS IS INCLUDED IN THIS VOLUME:
Bernard Baumohl, Lisa Beyer, Massimo Calabresi, Margaret Carlson, James Carney, Matthew Cooper, Howard Chua-Eoan, John Cloud, Jay Cocks, Adam Cohen, John Colmey, Richard Corliss, Andrea Dorfman, Philip Elmer-DeWitt, John F. Dickerson, Michael Duffy, Christopher John Farley, Michael Fathers, Jaime A. FlorCruz, Nancy Gibbs, Frank Gibney Jr., Elizabeth Gleick, Frederic Golden, Christine Gorman, Paul Gray, Karl Taro Greenfeld, John Greenwald, S.C. Gwynne, Nisid Hajari, Margot Hornblower, Walter Isaacson, Pico Iyer, Leon Jaroff, Daniel Kadlec, Jeffrey Kluger, Michael Krantz, Nadya Labi, Richard Lacayo, Michael D. Lemonick, David Liebhold, Steve Lopez, Belinda Luscombe, Scott MacLeod, J.F.O. McAllister, Terry McCarthy, Johanna McGeary, Tim McGirk, Andrew Meier, Jodie Morris, J. Madeleine Nash, Kate Noble, Daniel Okrent, Chris O'Malley, Michele Orecklin, Eric Pooley, Paul Quinn-Judge, Joshua Cooper Ramo, Romesh Ratnesar, Bill Saporito, Thomas Sancton, Richard Schickel, Teresita C. Schaffer, Elaine Shannon, Sin-ming Shaw, Anthony Spaeth, Joel Stein, Ron Stodghill II, Robert Sullivan, Chris Taylor, Dick Thompson, Mark Thompson, Karen Tumulty, David Van Biema, Yuri Zarakhovich, Richard Zoglin

SPECIAL THANKS TO:
Ames Adamson, Ken Baierlein, Robin Bierstedt, Sue Blair, Andy Blau, Jennifer Bomhoff, Sheila Charney, Anne Considine, Jay Colton, Suzanne Davis, Alison Ehrmann, Deena Goldblatt, Urbano DelValle, Dick Duncan, Linda Freeman, Arthur Hochstein, Ed Jamieson, Joe Lertola, Meghan Milkowski, Nancy Mynio, Rudi Papiri, Ron Plyman, Emily Rabin, Al Rufino, Betty Satterwhite, Ken Smith, Michele Stephenson, Miriam Winocour

We welcome your comments and suggestions about TIME Books. Please write to us at:
TIME Books • Attention: Book Editors • PO Box 11016 • Des Moines, IA 50336-1016

If you would like to order any of our hard-cover Collector Edition books, please call us at 1-800-327-6388, Monday through Friday, 7 a.m.–8 p.m. or Saturday, 7: a.m.–6 p.m. Central time.

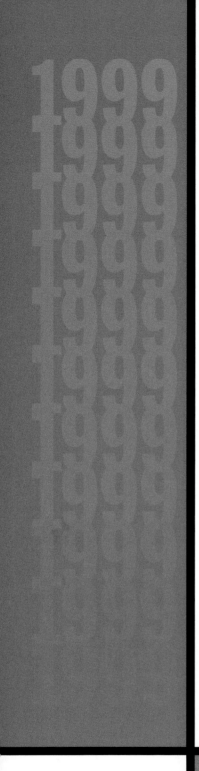

The year that ended with the

once-in-a-thousand years

rollover of all four digits on the

calendar brought the promise of

renewal, as candidates began

running hard to reach the White

House in 2000. It embraced

change, as Americans gave a

warm welcome to a new wave of

Hispanic artists. And it brought

tragedy in the form of school

shootings and the untimely

death of a President's son.

Yet with the economy bubbling

and the Internet remaking

society at an accelerating pace,

Americans found more to

celebrate than regret in 1999.

1999

2000
Millennium Edition

As the sun rose on the first day of a new millennium, people around the planet turned to the dawn with hopes of a brave new world. Defying doomsayers, the global celebration went off without a hitch: computers hummed, airplanes landed and took off, twins were born straddling millenniums, fireworks blasted, revelers partied, hangovers ensued ... well, you had to be there—and we were.

DEVOTEES OF DAWN: At the southernmost part of the Indian subcontinent, practitioners of a yogic ritual honor the sun god.

Images

It was a year when all Americans joined these students in walking the via dolorosa, the way of sorrows. Though crime rates fell, the pictures of horror were stronger, and they kept coming in a ghastly parade of mass murder—murder in schools and churches, murder in offices and day-care centers, murder in Colorado and Georgia, murder in Fort Worth and L.A.

IN MEMORIAM: A field of crosses commemorates the victims of the shootings at Columbine High School in the Denver suburb of Littleton.

Images

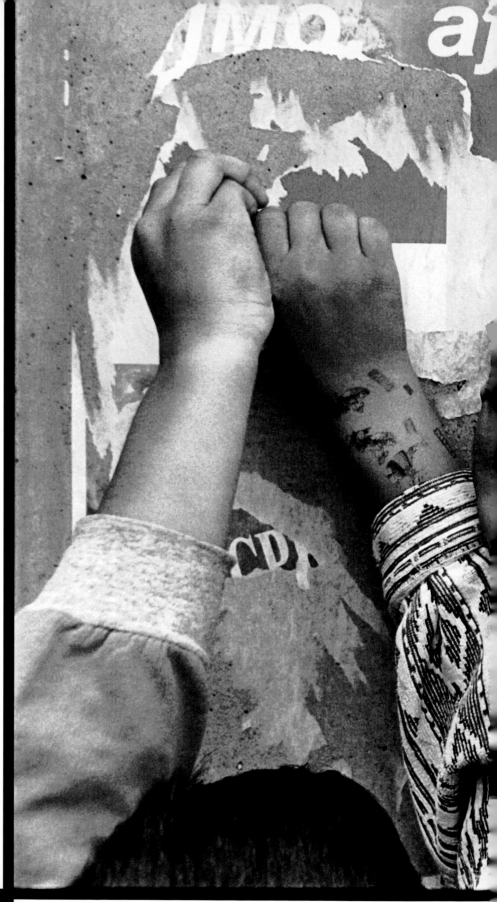

The hegira of the Kosovar refugees—more than 850,000 of them—reminded us that the urge to punish others simply because they are "different" was still alive. But for once, the strongman behind the savagery, Slobodan Milosevic, paid a price. His policies, his prestige—and his posters— were reduced to tatters.

SIC SEMPER TYRANNIS: Disillusioned Kosovars in Prizren deface a propaganda picture of Yugoslavia's President Milosevic.

Images

James Nachtwey—Magnum Photos

J. Pat Carter—AP–Wide World Photo

Every year brings its share of disasters, but in 1999 our purchase on the earth seemed more reliant than ever on nature's immense whims. Hurricanes battered North Carolina again and again, while earthquakes ravaged Turkey and Taiwan. And in Oklahoma, a mother sheltered her children under a highway overpass as a monster twister drew near.

TAKE COVER! Veteran storm chaser J. Pat Carter took this picture on May 3, 1999, outside Newcastle, Okla. The mother and children survived.

Images

Robert Beck—Sports Illustrated

How to top off a tournament that turned Americans—long resistant to the world's most popular sport—into soccer-crazed fanatics? Well, by taking your top off—as Brandi Chastain did, immediately after booting the goal that gave the United States women a thrilling win over China in the World Cup.

VICTORY! In this picture, shot through the goalposts, Chastain celebrates her winning kick in overtime. Final score: U.S. 5, China 4.

Images

TONY BLAIR & BILL CLINTON

*To celebrate NATO's 50th birthday
They blew out Belgrade: bombs away!*

WILLIAM REHNQUIST

*To the Hill a wise man came from afar
He didn't want to: he followed a Starr*

MICHAEL JORDAN

*What now for B-ball's retired great?
"Hey, honey, Millionaire's on at 8!"*

EDWARD & SOPHIE

*Why'd the fair lady marry her prince?
The triumph of hope over experience*

GEORGE LUCAS

*The critics declared that Menace stank
Alas! He cried all the way to the bank*

ABDULLAH OCALAN

*Man of no country, sad beyond words
Prisoner of Turks, beacon to Kurds*

EHUD BARAK

*You toppled Netanyahu, a stunning win
In fighting for peace, you honor Rabin*

MARLBORO MAN

*So long, podner, you're not the answer
We'll miss the horses but not the cancer*

RUDOLPH GIULIANI

*He hated "Sensation," called it unlawful:
"You call that art? I call it offal!"*

DANIEL ADEL FOR TIME
VICTOR JUHASZ FOR TIME
MARK FREDRICKSON FOR TIME
ANITA KUNZ FOR TIME
JOHN KASCHT FOR TIME
HUNGRY DOG STUDIOS FOR TIME
N. ASCENCIOS FOR TIME
TIM O'BRIEN FOR TIME
TIM O'BRIEN FOR TIME

WWF's Vince McMahon

His IPO was a champ at money making
The profits are real—the rest is faking

Mandela & Mbeki

Thabo takes over with his hero's blessing
Nelson, you swore: no second-guessing!

Paramount & CBS

Sumner Redstone rules MTV and VH1
Now make Dan Rather's network fun!

George W. Bush

No drug talk for him—that'd be stooping!
Why reply—and endorse your snooping?

Donald Trump

Watch out, White House! If he's elected
His name on your pillars will be erected

David E. Kelley

Wherefore this Bard's talent to amuse?
In his wife, he has a talent for a muse!

Elizabeth Dole

Her cash was a trickle, Bush's a Niagara
Take heart, Liddy: Bob's on Viagra!

AT&T's Michael Armstrong

This taunt to Ma Bell's rivals he hurled:
"With my wires, I could rule the world!"

Pete Rose

To win admission he's tried every tack
I betcha $50 he won't get a plaque

FIRST FAMILY 'DOS AND DON'TS

"Does she change her hair a lot?"

MADONNA, discussing the First Lady

"I admire all her hairdos. Personally, I've had the same one for the past 20 years."

ALICE STARR, Ken's wife, on Hillary Clinton

"Part of growing up is learning how to control one's impulses."

HILLARY CLINTON, introducing the President at a gun-control rally

"I like Bill Clinton. Do I think he's a total idiot? Yes."

HAROLD ICKES, former White House deputy chief of staff

"Did he look like Miles Davis? I don't know. But it's safe to say that he didn't look like Andy Gibb."

CHRIS ROCK, comedian, when asked if Jesus Christ was black

"During my service in the United States Congress, I took the initiative in creating the Internet."

AL GORE, on why Democrats should back him for President over Bill Bradley

"During my service in the United States Congress, I took the initiative in creating the paper clip."

SENATOR TRENT LOTT, the majority leader, in a humorous riposte

"I learned interesting things from James Caan, like how to blow my nose without a handkerchief ... You almost never see Emma Thompson do it."

HUGH GRANT, actor, on what he learned while making his new film

"God almighty, take the vote and get it over with!"

RICHARD DOUGLAS LLAMAS, spectator, shouting during the impeachment trial

MUCH ADO ABOUT MADELEINE

"See what happens when you let men into the Cabinet?"

MADELEINE ALBRIGHT, Secretary of State, about two male colleagues discussing clothes shopping

"Thank God we sent George Mitchell and not Madeleine [Albright] to Ireland. We'd be bombing them this morning."

SENATOR ERNEST HOLLINGS, on brokering peace in Northern Ireland

"She was not attempting to fish ... She was attempting to cast."

An aide to MADELEINE ALBRIGHT, after the Secretary of State angled for salmon in Alaska

"You always have champagne before shows. Always. Even at 10 in the morning. It got to the point one time when we were, 'We're not going out without any champagne.' Terrible."

KATE MOSS, waif, but not naïf, on her former drinking problem

"Adhere to the basic economic system with public ownership dominant and diverse forms of ownership developing side-by-side, and 'to each according to his work' as the main distribution form and with other forms as well!"

SLOGAN, one of 50 the Chinese were permitted to chant during the People's Republic's 50th anniversary

"First you're painted into a corner, then you're hung out to dry, and finally you're framed."

WARREN CHRISTOPHER, former Secretary of State, on how having a portrait painted is like working in Washington

"He does this funny thing with his lip."

LUCIANA MORAD, on her son by Mick Jagger

"If anyone ever tells you, 'It's not about the money'—it's about the money."

DALE BUMPERS, former Senator, defending Bill Clinton

"Women pay for contraceptives, and insurance companies pay for Viagra. What's wrong with this picture?"

Representative JAMES C. GREENWOOD, introducing a bill to extend health coverage to include contraceptives

"Great brother"

The Chinese term for Viagra

"My son saw a full-grown cow that had been impaled on a broken power pole. Just like a shish kebab."

JEANNETTE RALSTON, resident of Bridge Creek, Okla., after a tornado

"Yasser Arafat … is like a stripper. But the stripper, with all the clothes she takes off, gets more and more beautiful. Yasser Arafat, with every concession that he makes … gets more ugly."

MUSTAFA TLASS, Syrian Defense Minister, on Arafat's negotiations with Israel

"I can't. My husband's famous."

MICHELLE PFEIFFER, spouse of David E. Kelley (creator of *Ally McBeal, The Practice, Chicago Hope*), on going into hiding

"After these last six years, I've got charisma fatigue."

DICK ARMEY, House majority leader, on who wins the charisma battle, Al Gore or George W. Bush

"It's easy to sing, but it's not easy to do."

POPE JOHN PAUL II, after a crowd sang a traditional Polish greeting, *May You Live 100 Years*

"I now have a 7-year-old boy and a 9-year-old boy, so all I can say is, I apologize. Now I know what you guys were talking about."

MATT GROENING, creator of *The Simpsons*, responding to complaints that Bart Simpson is a bad role model

DISSES OF THE YEAR

"Who is this coming? Oh, a famous actor. Too bad. What I need is a doctor."

HATIXHE AJETI, a Kosovar, on seeing Richard Gere visiting her refugee camp

"People who learn history from Spielberg movies should not tell us how to live our lives."

JADRANKA DJORDJEVIC, former worker at the U.S. embassy in Belgrade

"Promoting Larry Summers to be U.S. Treasury Secretary is like sending Typhoid Mary into a maternity ward."

STEVE FORBES, G.O.P. presidential candidate

"A black man voting for the Republicans makes about as much sense as a chicken voting for Colonel Sanders."

J.C. ("BUDDY") WATTS SR., father of J.C. Watts Jr., the only black Republican in Congress

"I think she is the checkout person at the local market."

JANET RENO, U.S. Attorney General, quoting a couple she overheard trying to think how they knew her

"He looked like he was the college president of the University of Mars."

PAUL BEGALA, former Clinton adviser, on Steve Forbes

"We haven't had this much excitement … since Banjo Greenfield's son Dozer towed his double-wide through town."

MATT MAJOR, citizen of Skaneateles, N.Y., on the Clintons' vacation there

PERSONS OF THE MILLENNIUM
The prime movers of mankind's past 1,000 years

How to go about finding the one individual who best embodies the disparate themes of the 20th century? To help establish the criteria that distinguish a Person of the Century, TIME's editors selected a person to represent the dominant impulses of each of the preceding nine centuries of the 2nd millennium. The results ranged broadly across cultures, from a Mongol warrior to an Islamic sheik, from an Italian painter to an English Queen to a German inventor.

WILLIAM THE CONQUEROR seized power in England, then pioneered a state bureaucracy that ensured stability for his small nation amid Europe's chaos .

SALADIN defeated the Christian crusaders but did not savage them. Tolerant, humane and just, he fostered Islamic culture and art.

GENGHIS KHAN swept through Asia like an apocalypse, linking the Pacific Ocean to the Black Sea.

GIOTTO broke through the stilted conventions of medieval painting to place humanity at art's core.

JOHANN GUTENBERG kindled an information revolution and a religious upheaval with his great invention, the printing press.

QUEEN ELIZABETH I was a goddess of the Reformation who presided over her country's renaissance, defeated Spain—then Europe's greatest power— and set Britain on its way to becoming an empire.

ISAAC NEWTON offered mankind a new vision, a miraculously predictable and rational clockwork creation held together by universal gravitation and by his elegant laws of force and motion.

THOMAS JEFFERSON gave the Enlightenment its most eloquent and succinct political expression, lifting humanity into a higher orbit.

THOMAS EDISON brought forth inventions that hurtled Western society into today's high-tech environment.

THE TIME 100

Who mattered most? We select the key players of our century—and those who changed the course of our millennium

LEADERS & REVOLUTIONARIES

David Ben-Gurion
Israel's first Prime Minister

Winston Churchill
British Prime Minister

Mohandas Gandhi
Father of modern India

Mikhail Gorbachev
Soviet reformer

Adolf Hitler, *German dictator*

Ho Chi Minh, *First President of North Vietnam*

Pope John Paul II
Religious leader

Ayatullah R. Khomeini
Leader of Iran's revolution

Martin Luther King Jr.
Civil rights leader

Vladimir Ilyich Lenin
Founder of the Soviet Union

Nelson Mandela
South African President

ARTISTS & ENTERTAINERS

Louis Armstrong
Jazz musician

Lucille Ball, *TV star*

The Beatles, *Rock musicians*

Marlon Brando, *Actor*

Coco Chanel, *Designer*

Charlie Chaplin, *Film pioneer and comic genius*

Le Corbusier, *Architect*

Bob Dylan, *Folk musician*

T.S. Eliot, *Poet*

Aretha Franklin, *Soul musician*

Martha Graham
Dancer and choreographer

Jim Henson, *Puppeteer and creator of TV's Muppets*

James Joyce, *Novelist*

Pablo Picasso, *Artist*

Rodgers & Hammerstein
Broadway showmen

The 100 Most Influential

Mao Zedong
Leader of communist China

Ronald Reagan
U.S. President

Eleanor Roosevelt
U.S. First Lady

Franklin Delano Roosevelt
U.S. President and architect of the New Deal

Theodore Roosevelt
U.S. President, environmentalist

Margaret Sanger
Birth-control crusader

Margaret Thatcher
British Prime Minister

Unknown Tiananmen Square Rebel, *Idealist*

Lech Walesa
Polish union organizer

Bart Simpson
Animated activist

Frank Sinatra, *Singer*

Steven Spielberg, *Moviemaker*

Igor Stravinsky
Classical musician

Oprah Winfrey
TV talk-show host

BUILDERS & TITANS

Stephen Bechtel
Construction magnate

Leo Burnett
Advertising genius

Willis Carrier, *Pioneer of air-conditioning systems*

Walt Disney, *Film pioneer, founder of a media empire*

Henry Ford
Founder of Ford Motor Co.

Bill Gates
Co-founder of Microsoft

A.P. Giannini, *Architect of nationwide banking*

Ray Kroc, *Hamburger meister*

Estee Lauder
Cosmetics tycoon

William Levitt
Creator of suburbia

Lucky Luciano
Criminal mastermind

Louis B. Mayer
Hollywood mogul

Charles Merrill, *Advocate of the small investor*

Akio Morita
Co-founder of Sony

Walter Reuther, *Labor leader*

Pete Rozelle
Football commissioner

David Sarnoff
Father of broadcasting

Juan Trippe
Aviation entrepreneur

Sam Walton
Wal-Mart dynamo

Thomas Watson Jr.
IBM president

SCIENTISTS & THINKERS

Leo Baekeland
Plastics pioneer

The Leakey Family
Anthropologists

Jean Piaget, *Child psychologist*

Jonas Salk, *Virologist*

William Shockley
Solid-state physicist

Alan Turing, *Computer scientist*

James Watson & Francis Crick
Molecular biologists

Ludwig Wittgenstein
Philosopher

The Wright Brothers
Visionary aviators

HEROES & ICONS

Muhammad Ali
Heavyweight boxing champion

The American G.I.
A soldier for freedom

Diana, *Princess of Wales*

Anne Frank
Diarist and Holocaust victim

Billy Graham, *Evangelist*

Che Guevara, *Guerrilla leader*

Edmund Hillary &
Tenzing Norgay, *Conquerors of Mount Everest*

Helen Keller
Champion of the disabled

The Kennedys
Political dynasty

People of the 20th Century

Tim Berners-Lee
Pioneer of World Wide Web

Rachel Carson
Environmentalist

Albert Einstein
Revolutionary physicist

Philo Farnsworth, *Inventor of electronic television*

Enrico Fermi
Atomic physicist

Alexander Fleming
Bacteriologist

Sigmund Freud
Psychoanalyst

Robert Goddard
Rocket scientist

Kurt Gödel, *Mathematician*

Edwin Hubble, *Astronomer*

John Maynard Keynes
Economist

Bruce Lee
Actor and martial-arts star

Charles Lindbergh
Transatlantic aviator

Harvey Milk
Gay-rights leader

Marilyn Monroe, *Actress*

Emmeline Pankhurst
Suffragist

Rosa Parks
Civil rights torchbearer

Pele, *Soccer star*

Jackie Robinson
Baseball player

Andrei Sakharov
Soviet dissident

Mother Teresa
Missionary nun

Bill Wilson, *Alcoholics Anonymous founder*

PERSON OF THE CENTURY
The prime mover of our era—and two runners-up

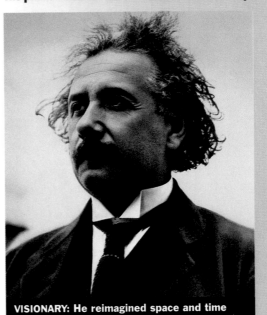

VISIONARY: He reimagined space and time

ALBERT EINSTEIN As the century's greatest thinker, as an immigrant who fled from oppression to freedom, as a political idealist, the great physicist best embodies what historians will regard as significant about the 20th century. And as a philosopher with faith in both science and in the beauty of God's handiwork, he personifies the legacy that has been bequeathed to the next century. The name that will prove most enduring from our amazing era will be that of Albert Einstein: genius, political refugee, humanitarian, locksmith of the mysteries of the atom and the universe.

MOHANDAS GANDHI taught us that we should value the civil liberties and individual rights of other human beings; he fought oppression without violence, preaching tolerance and pluralism.

FRANKLIN D. ROOSEVELT helped save capitalism from its most serious challenge, then rallied the power of free people to defeat fascism.

RUNNERS-UP: They fought to make men free

What a party! From Singapore to Stockholm, Times Square to Tiananmen Square, it may have been the single greatest celebration in the history of the world, crossing lines of culture, religion and race. The question going in: Will the dastardly Y2K computer bug stop the world in its tracks? The question coming out: Which city put on the best party? Top picks included upstarts Sydney and Paris, which may have topped longtime champ Times Square.

G'DAY! Gearing up for the 2000 Olympic Games, Sydney Harbor exploded with one of the planet's showiest bashes.

2000

2000
THE MILLENNIUM

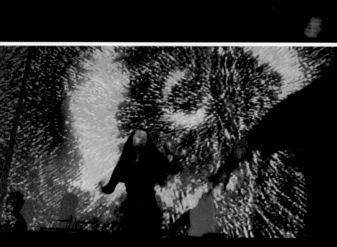

"Tonight We're Gonna Party Like It's 1999"

Champagne or vodka? Fireworks or sky lanterns? China's Great Wall, Moscow's Red Square or Egypt's pyramids? The question as the calendar turned to the magic numerals 2000 wasn't *whether* you would party—it was how and where. The revelers included Queen Elizabeth II, above, and Nelson Mandela, facing page, who beams from his former prison cell on South Africa's Robben Island. Scattered among the Times Square celebrators—many of them wearing 2000 specs—are scenes of parties from around the world. The dancers in a disco bubble pool, above left, are in Bali, Indonesia; below them, Taiwanese release 10,000 sky lanterns in Taipei. Below left, drummers welcome the new century in Ho Chi Minh City, Vietnam. At bottom center of facing page, dancers get in the mood at an all-night rave in Santa Monica, Calif., that was broadcast live on the Internet.

Midnight, Four Digits Rotate, and Sparks Fly

You would never know it from the picture at left, but just days before the New Year, France was slammed by once-in-a-century storms that might have stopped its once-in-a-millennium party. Parts of the nation had to greet the new century as they had the last— without electricity. But don't count out Gallic joie de vivre: Paris played host to one of the world's most spectacular events, transforming its great 19th century totem, the Eiffel Tower, into a geyser of light. Six hours later, New York City's Times Square entered the magic midnight hour with the largest gathering in its history. The city's bash, by the numbers: close to 2 million people, 130,000 free souvenirs (including long red balloons and Mylar rainbow wigs), 8,000 police officers, 6,000 lbs. of confetti, 48 bomb threats (all of them false)—and one helluva party.

Y2K:
THE BUG THAT ROARED

And roared. And then—happily—fizzled. After a year of computer-bug fears
and a month of terrorism warnings, everything was Y2OK on New Year's Day

Y2K WAS A FABLE FOR OUR TIME: HAL THE COMPUTER recast as a billion bugs, his omnipotent malevolence replaced by our own innocent oversight. Technology had become so all-encompassing and incomprehensible, the fable began, that we had unwittingly lost control of it. So the smallest thing, our human habit of hiply referring to years by the last two digits, was going to topple this electronic house of cards, sending planes crashing to the ground, nukes leaping from their silos, lights flickering into darkness and all of humanity hurtling back to a time much earlier than the 1900 our computers would believe it was. It was a cleansing fantasy, a dream of ridding ourselves of the heavy yoke of overcivilization and going back to a time simple enough for us to understand.

So at 4:30 a.m. on Dec. 31, in Lisbon, Ohio, fable believers Bruce and Diane Eckhart awoke and immersed themselves in technology for what they believed was the last time, turning on their two televisions, dialing up the Internet and clicking on their shortwave radio to monitor the first Y2K rollover, in Kiribati. Since 1997 the Eckharts had been stockpiling food, staging surprise drills, practicing with firearms, turning savings into gold coins and studying rudimentary dentistry and field medicine. "So far, it's just a minor power outage in New Zealand," Diane reported, before uttering words you don't often hear: "But we've heard nothing about Guam; it's kind of disturbing."

As the day wore on, and news reports showed that not even China was having problems, their daughter Danielle,

12, was the first to lose interest. "Whatever happens, happens," she said, after singing along to a Sheryl Crow tape. "We won't have to go grocery shopping for a while." And while Bruce, 45, was still talking about being wary of strangers from neighboring Youngstown coming to loot his stash, Diane, 42, was already contemplating their massive store of canned food. "I'm going to save on groceries," she announced, determined to eat their 12 cans of Spam, disaster or not. "I can't decide if I'm going to buy a Jacuzzi or a new computer with the money."

In Ontario, Bruce Beach, who began constructing a bunker of 42 buried school buses 18 years ago, watched astounded as city after city passed into modernity with nary a scratch. And MTV Online, as if to mock it all, was showing a live video feed of the six kids it set up in a campy Y2K bunker under a building in Manhattan.

Almost as interested in world rollovers as the bunkered down were the U.S. and Russian military officers at Peterson Air Force Base, the now permanent Center for Year 2000 Strategic Stability. Officers from both sides of the cold peace, who were there to make sure no nukes accidentally went off, labored to keep busy, channel surfing among CNN and other news shows and investigating Russian Internet fare. The only old-school touch was the hotline phones: black for Moscow, white for the U.S.

When the clocks changed in Moscow and no computer bugs were reported, the Russian team applauded, and U.S. Major General Thomas Goslin Jr. congratulated Russian group leader Colonel Sergey Kaplin. He may have deserved even more congratulations. Russia spent $4 million on Y2K military preparations while the U.S. spent nearly $4 billion. In fact, Americans spent an estimated $100 billion to be ready on all fronts, from telecommunications to sewage treatment. It will probably remain unclear whether that was money partly wasted or money that saved us from a meltdown—take your pick.

The FAA confidently sent its chief, Jane Garvey, flying from Washington to Dallas during the key hour of midnight Greenwich Mean Time. The only surprising thing about the flight was that the FAA chief had to fly coach. Fear itself was virtually nonexistent on Friday, Dec. 31, with almost no one making a last-minute ATM run, leaving the $50 billion of extra cash the Federal Reserve had printed for the occasion to be turned into mulch. In Japan, Prime Minister Keizo Obuchi tried to backpedal from weeks of warnings to stockpile food and water. He had even declared a three-day emergency holiday. A country that has been burned as badly by its faith in technology over the past decade as Japan has every reason to be careful.

So as Apocalypse Not struck around the globe, people everywhere celebrated, despite the fact that many societies follow completely different calendars, and despite the fact that some people insisted on pointing out that the millennium doesn't really start until Jan. 1, 2001. But while the hard-liners may have been technically correct, people made merry because the most famous odometer mankind has ever created was displaying three zeroes in a row. It's exciting enough when it happens to your own car; when it happens to the world, it makes you downright giddy. ∎

THE FINAL FEAR: NEW YEAR'S EVIL
Terrorism, not computer bugs, was the real unknown

After years of warnings about the potential for a technological meltdown caused by the Y2K computer bug, the real concern among security agents as the millennium approached was terrorism. U.S. officials live in dread of an NSSE—the Disneyesque abbreviation for a national-security special event that triggers special precautions. As the end of the year approached, a flood of threats erupted in every corner of the globe. The State Department issued two warnings about possible overseas attacks. The FBI raised the temperature with an alert for mail bombs.

The thermometer peaked with the arrest of a 32-year-old Algerian named Ahmed Ressam. Trying to sneak into the U.S. from Canada, he was caught by luck as much as diligence, for the 3,000-mile-plus northern border of the U.S. is as porous as Swiss cheese. Around 6 p.m. on Dec. 14, Diana Dean, an inspector at Port Angeles, Wash., went over to a man in a rented Chrysler; her attention was piqued by his shaking hands. Not only did he carry several false identity cards alongside his

ON ALERT: The arrest of Ressam, right, sparked an increase in security at the U.S.–Canadian border

Canadian passport (in the name of Benni Noris), but also the well of his car trunk revealed a chilling cache: 10 plastic bags loaded with enough material to create a bomb big enough to take out the Seattle Space Needle. He was carrying a plane ticket to London, via New York City—a potential target, or an escape route?

The suspect, quickly identified, was well known to officials in Paris, who said he belonged to "an extremely dangerous network of Islamic fundamentalists" intent on an "international holy war." U.S. officials suspected he might be a free-lancing foot soldier for Osama bin Laden, the Saudi-born terror kingpin charged with organizing the embassy bombings that killed 224 in Kenya and Tanzania in 1998. Border security was immediately tightened, and America's New Year's Eve party went off without a hitch—except in a spooked Seattle, which canceled its celebration.

Photo-illustration for TIME by Aaron Goodman. Photos: Jeremy Walker—Tony Stone, Jim Nations—DDB Stock, Jack Swenson

Every time a seismic shift takes place in our economy, there are people who feel the vibrations long before the rest of us do, vibrations so strong they demand action—action that can seem rash. Jeffrey Preston Bezos felt those vibrations when he first peered into the maze of connected computers called the World Wide Web and envisioned a company, Amazon, that would help us shop, communicate and live closer together. For helping build a foundation of the future, Jeff Bezos is TIME's Person of the Year 1999.

Person of the Year

JEFF BEZOS LOVES BEING ON THE move. He sits in the back of a white van, beaming as usual, surrounded by an entourage of lanky young lieutenants from Amazon.com, the Web's biggest retail store and, someday, if Bezos gets it right, Earth's Biggest Store. The early-morning landscape of southeast Kansas hustles by: wood-frame houses, trailers, motels with lots of pickup trucks in their parking lots, a Kum & Go convenience store, cow pastures and the dull, forever flatness of the prairie. You've heard of places described as cow towns? Coffeyville was actually labeled Cow Town on maps on account of the stockyards here. In the 1860s the name was changed to honor Colonel James A. Coffey, who set up a trading post here, selling stuff to Native Americans.

used. The rest is stretch space, set aside to make room for the ongoing e-commerce revolution.

If all goes according to Bezos' daring—some might say outlandish—plan, this warehouse will be at capacity within the next few years and will handle everything: washing machines, cars, rubber gaskets, Prozac, exercise machines, marmalade, model airplanes—everything but firearms and certain live animals. You name it, Amazon will sell it. "Anything," says Bezos, "with a capital *A*." And that's the point: Jeffrey Preston Bezos is trying to assemble nothing less than Earth's Biggest Selection of Goods, then put all of it on his website for people to find and buy. Not just physical things that you can touch, but services too, such as banking, insurance, travel.

It's incredibly risky. How elastic is the Amazon brand name? How much can you expand it until it simply explodes and becomes meaningless to consumers? And how long can the money hold out? Bezos has already burned through a bank's worth of cash with no sign of slowing down. If anything, he's upping the ante—according to estimates, the company's net loss could be $350 million in 1999 alone. Yet during the first two weeks of December,

MAN IN MOTION

Jeff Bezos has a dream: Amazon.com will be Earth's biggest seller of everything

Today's frontier is hidden from the physical world, burbling and buzzing along the interconnected wires, routers and computers of the Net. But the possibilities for trade are far more fabulous than could ever have been imagined 100—or even 10—years ago. That's where Bezos comes in. His van passes an airfield, heads down a two-lane road and pulls into a long driveway that leads to the biggest warehouse you've ever seen. The place is known as the Coffeyville Distribution Center, and Bezos (pronounced *Bay-zos*), who's never been here before, is giggling with glee. He tells the driver to stop so he can snap a picture of a workman pounding a HELP WANTED sign into the turf. Bezos, 35, a meticulous documentarian, is worried that his life is scrolling by too fast to remember, a life that is so fantastic as to verge on the unbelievable.

Here in Coffeyville is one piece of the proof that Bezos' early and fervent belief in the Internet—that it would rock retailing, that it would change the way we live—stands as one of the more prescient assumptions ever

**ODDBALL?
Not really.
Bezos is a
regular guy
who enjoys
a challenge**

made by a businessperson. "We're trying to build something lasting," Bezos says, looking at this 850,000-sq.-ft. monument to free trade. The warehouse is stocked with books, CDs, TVs, stereos, video games, software, toys. And yet only 10% of the area is being

with holiday sales booming, Amazon's stock price soared to $94. The stock has split three times. Sales are expected to crest $1 billion in 1999.

What's driving the boom? Bezos & Co. conceived an entirely new way of thinking about the ancient art of retailing, automating as much as possible a complex process that starts when you hit the patent-protected "1-Click" buy technology and ends when your purchase is delivered to your door. The Coffeyville center is part of a nationwide distribution network specially designed to handle e-commerce. Half a dozen warehouses like it have been strategically placed in low- or no-sales-tax states around the U.S.— 3 million sq. ft., at a cost of $200 million—and are built to do what traditional warehouses can't do: deliver items directly and efficiently to customers rather than by pallet to retail stores. Billboard-size banners festoon its aisles and walls. One lists the company's Six Core Values: "customer obsession, ownership, bias for action, frugality, high hiring bar and innovation." It's like the Cultural Revolution meets Sam Walton. It's dotcommunism!

Some people must be genetically predisposed to explore the frontiers. Bezos' family can trace its American roots to the turn of the 19th century, when a colorful, 6-ft. 4-in. pioneer named Colonel Robert Hall moved to San Antonio, Texas, from his home in Tennessee. Jeff's mother, as smart, headstrong and pioneering as anyone in the clan,

YOUNG COWPOKE: Bezos spent happy summers on a ranch in Texas before graduating from Princeton in 1986

THE FAMILY WAY: Bezos with wife MacKenzie, above, and with stepfather Mike, who raised him, at left

PHOTOGRAPHS COURTESY THE BEZOS FAMILY

married young and gave birth to Jeff on Jan. 12, 1964, when she was 17. The marriage lasted about a year. Jeff has neither memory of nor interest in his biological father. "My real father is the guy who raised me," he says. That guy is Mike Bezos, a Cuban refugee who moved to the U.S. by himself when he was 15 years old, with nothing more than two shirts and a pair of pants. Taken under wing by a Catholic mission, Mike learned English and made his way to the University of Albuquerque. While working the night shift as a clerk at a bank, he met Jackie, a fellow employee; they married when Jeff was four.

Jeff was an extremely smart child. Fed up with sleeping in a crib, the toddler found a screwdriver and reduced his jail to its component parts. He built models, worked a Radio Shack electronics kit to the nubs and endlessly tinkered with stuff. In high school in Miami—his father, an engineer with Exxon, moved the family several times—Jeff became the valedictorian. He didn't drink, do drugs or even swear. People liked him anyway. And almost every summer, he headed for his grandfather's 25,000-acre ranch in Cotulla, Texas. It was the perfect antidote to the brainy world he inhabited the rest of the year. On the ranch he would ride horses, brand cattle with a LAZY G and fix windmills.

Bezos graduated from Princeton University, majoring in electrical engineering and computer science. His first job out of school was at Fitel, a start-up that was building a network to handle international financial trades. He spent about two years there, worked about the same amount of time at Bankers Trust, then got an interview at D.E. Shaw, an unusual firm of brainiacs who advise major corporations on technological strategy. Over time, Bezos became a specialist in researching business opportunities in insurance, software and then the booming Internet.

If you had to pick a single *eureka!* moment, a time when suddenly everything became clear about what the future had in mind for Jeff Bezos, it was on a May day in 1994. The 30-year-old was sitting at the computer in his 39th-floor office in midtown Manhattan, exploring the still immature Internet, and he came across this statistic: the Internet was growing at a rate of 2,300% a year.

"It was a wake-up call," Bezos says. "I started thinking, O.K., what kind of business opportunity might there be here?" His answer: "To be a complete first mover in e-commerce." He researched mail-order companies, figuring that things that sold well by mail would do well online. He made a list of the Top 20 mail-order products and looked for where he could create "the most value for customers … something that simply cannot be done any other way."

And that's what ultimately led to books. There weren't any huge mail-order book catalogs simply because a good catalog would contain thousands, if not millions of listings. The catalog would need to be as big as a phone book—too expensive to mail. That, of course, made it perfect for the Internet, the ideal container for limitless information. And books, it turned out, were already among the most highly databased items on the planet, ready to be put online.

Bezos discussed his plan with his wife MacKenzie, a fellow Princeton graduate; they had met at Shaw, where she worked as a researcher. An English-literature major at the university, she had been novelist Toni Morrison's assistant and had begun a novel of her own. She assured her husband that she was all for the adventure.

Bezos told his first investors—family and friends: "I think there's a 70% chance you're going to lose all your money, so don't invest unless you can afford to lose it." His parents ponied up $300,000, a huge chunk of their retire-

were onto something much bigger than we ever dared to hope." The company grew and grew and grew. After its initial public offering in May 1997, the stock began to move too, propelling Bezos' personal wealth into the tens of millions, then into the hundreds of millions. As of December 1999, his shares were worth more than $10 billion.

Ah, but money … Who cares about that? Bezos has cashed in less than $25 million worth of his stock. He and his wife live in a sprawling, single-story modern home in the suburbs north of Seattle. "At some point," he says, giving MacKenzie a hug as they stand around in its kitchen, "we want to do philanthropic work that's highly leveraged

In 1994 Amazon started up in Jeff Bezos' garage, on desks made from doors

ment savings. "We didn't invest in Amazon," says his mother, "we invested in Jeff." The ROJ—return on Jeff—was substantial. Today, with a 6% stake, they're billionaires.

On July 4 weekend, Jeff and MacKenzie flew out to Fort Worth, Texas, bid goodbye to his family and headed for Seattle—a city near one of America's two biggest book wholesalers and chock-full of the kinds of Net-savvy people he would need to hire. MacKenzie handled the driving, while Jeff tapped out a business plan on a laptop computer.

The most important person Bezos hired was probably the first: Shel Kaphan, a brilliant programmer in Santa Clara, Calif., and veteran of a dozen start-ups, many of them failures. Their "company" was headquartered in a modest two-bedroom home that Jeff and MacKenzie rented in Bellevue, a Seattle suburb. They converted the garage into a work space and brought in three Sun workstations; extension cords snaked from every available outlet in the house to the garage. To save money, Bezos went to Home Depot and bought three wooden doors. Using angle brackets and 2-by-4s, he hammered together three desks, at a cost of $60 each. (That frugality continues at Amazon to this day; every employee sits behind a door masquerading as a desk.)

By June 1995 a rudimentary website had been created on a hidden site and 300 friends and family members were sworn to secrecy and invited to crash-test it. "The first time I saw the site, I said to myself, 'Wow, this is it,'" recalls David Shaw, Bezos' former boss. It was simple and functional. Kaphan's code was incredibly elegant and streamlined, allowing pages to be delivered without delay. On July 16, 1995, Amazon.com opened its site to the world. Bezos simply told all 300 beta testers to spread the word. In less than a month's time, without any press, Amazon sold books in all 50 states and 45 other countries. "Within the first few days, I knew this was going to be huge," says Bezos. "It was obvious that we

… Say you want to solve world hunger. If you think in terms of a five-year time frame, you get really depressed; it's an intractable problem. But if you say, Let's see how we could solve this in 100 years—it's a problem because you'll be dead by then, but the solution becomes more tractable."

"Anyway," he adds quickly, self-deprecatingly, in probably the same way he told people Amazon had only a 30% chance of success, "it'll be a long time before we build a lasting company." And he laughs and laughs and laughs. ■

PHOTO-ILLUSTRATION FOR TIME BY AARON GOODMAN

MERRILY, MERRILY: After Amazon, Bezos hopes to master philanthropy

CRUISING INSIDE AMAZON

It's like a three-ring circus that adds more rings each day

BMVP2000

THE PHRASE SITS THERE ON THE GIANT MONITORS, AND 2,000 Amazonians packing the Seattle Westin for a quarterly "all hands" meeting listen raptly while Jeff Bezos explains what it means. There are two types of businesses, he tells the troops: baby businesses, which need growth and feeding, and adult businesses, which must pay their own way. This brings him to *B*, *M* and *V*, which stand for books, music and video, Amazon's three oldest product lines. And the *P* is today's news, for this trinity is nearing adulthood. "By the end of the year 2000," Bezos says, "we're going to make them profitable."

The troops are silent. Stunned. Amazon, profitable? It's autumn 1999. For years these people have been racing toward a horizon that no one, save perhaps their utopian-futurist boss, even really sees. They know much of the Silicon Valley/Wall Street/media complex believes the commodification of online retailing will lay their company to waste. Amazon the Web's golden child, darling of NASDAQ day traders who raise its market cap even faster than the company bleeds money, is also Amazon the avatar of all that may be ephemeral and fraudulent about the dotcom revolution. Now Bezos has named a date one year hence that will be the time they find out whether they're going to make it or not. A chance, after all those 16-hr. workdays, for the company actually to fail. Their fearless leader notes their angst and offers a beneficent smile.

"You can cheer," Bezos says. So the assembled Netheads cheer. Imagine that! Amazon, profitable.

This is ground zero of the New Economy? At age five, Earth's Biggest Bookstore is now Earth's Biggest Selection, in keeping with Bezos' plan for world domination. Meaning what, exactly? Well, in a sense, Amazon isn't about technology or even commerce. Any fool can open an online store. The trick is showing millions of customers such a good time that they come back every few days for the next 50 years. Amazon is, like every other site on the Web, a content play.

Thus Amazon now has an editorial department, a rich stew of writers, academics and other liberal-arts types. A century ago, millions of brave souls crossed the Atlantic to the land of opportunity. Now their descendants are making their own western migration, and these days many of them are landing in Seattle. Kerry Fried (books) was an editor for the *Village Voice Literary Supplement.* James Marcus (books) was a literary critic. Jenny Brown (video) has an M.F.A. in creative writing. Simon Leake (video) was a doctoral candidate in Renaissance studies. "I know so many people who got their Ph.D. and cannot find work," Leake says. "They're all going into business or journalism."

Or both. The editorial folks' job is to create opinionated, entertaining guides to Amazon products: reviews, interviews, gift ideas, and what have you. They spend their days agonizing over, say, which offbeat and obscure film documentary to name the Pick of the Week and maybe only occasionally pondering the spiritual implications of this whole writing-for-a-shopping-mall gig.

For three years, defining Amazon was easy: it sold books. Then it sold books, music and videos. Now it sells toys, tools, consumer electronics and software as well. Then there are the equity stakes in start-ups like drugstore.com, pets.com and Gear.com, and struggling eBay-wannabe divisions: zShops and Auctions. Who are these guys now? What does Amazon represent? And will the company's more than 13 million customers stick around for power drills and wide-screen TVs? "No one's sure where all this is going," says Carrie Johnson, an analyst with Forrester Research and an Amazon optimist. "Initiatives like zShops and Auctions are distracting to the brand. They need a tab on the home page that says, OTHER CRAP."

What Johnson and other believers agree on is the wisdom of the company's relentless reinvestment in new markets in lieu of banking premature profits. Bezos' strategic analysis goes like this: customer acquisition is only going to get harder tomorrow, so you have to grab every customer you can today. For those 13 million customers translate into dominant market share. And dominant market share means the power, for instance, to strong-arm suppliers for better deals, which could lead to profitability: BMVP2000.

So, since mid-1998, the company has grown from one online store to more than a dozen, and from 1,100 to more than 5,000 love-it-or-leave-it, multitasking nomads. Amazon offices are scattered across Seattle: the flagship Art Deco Pacific Medical Center, the Pike Street skyscraper, the original Columbia building and so on. Stunning views of Lake Washington and Puget Sound are the only luxury the spartan corporate aesthetic allows. Employees, packed two to a bare-walled office, work at Bezos' trademark desks made of old doors with legs stuck on them.

THE PICKER: John Edwards fills book orders at the Seattle warehouse

Location: http://www.jeffbezosispersonoftheyear.time.com/

FROM YOUR MOUSE TO YOUR HOUSE

What goes on behind the scenes when you place an order at Amazon.com

1 You order three items, and a computer in Seattle takes charge

A computer assigns your order—a book, a game and a digital camera—to one of Amazon's seven U.S. distribution centers, five of which it opened this year. With 3 million sq. ft., Amazon has 1.5 times the floor space of the Empire State Building.

Seattle ✪ 93,000 sq. ft.

Grand Forks, N.D. ○ 130,000

New Castle, Del. ○ 202,000

Fernley, Nev. ○ 332,650

Coffeyville, Kans. ○ 750,000

Campbellsville, Ky. ○ 770,000

McDonough, Ga. ○ 800,000

3 Your items are put into crates on moving belts

Each item goes into a large green crate that contains many customers' orders. When full, the crates ride a series of conveyor belts that winds more than 10 miles through the plant at a constant speed of 2.9 ft. per sec. The bar code on each item is scanned 15 times, by machines and by many of the 600 full-time workers, all of whom get Amazon stock options.

ISBN 0-7894-3512-8 90000>
9 780789 435125

4 All three items converge in a chute, and then inside a box

All of the crates arrive at a central point where bar codes are matched with order numbers to determine who gets what. Your three items end up in a 3-ft.-wide chute—one of several thousand—and are placed into a cardboard box with a new bar code that identifies your order.

5 Any gifts you've chosen are wrapped by hand

Amazon trains an élite group of gift wrappers to "make it look like Mom's." Each worker processes 30 packages an hour (those who fail are reassigned to other jobs). For its busiest season yet, Amazon's warehouses are stocked with 4.4 million yards of ribbon and 7.8 million sq. ft. of wrapping paper—which if laid flat would more than cover Disneyland.

6 The box is packed, taped, weighed and labeled before leaving the warehouse in a truck

The McDonough plant was designed to ship as many as 200,000 pieces a day. About 60% of orders are shipped via the U.S. Postal Service; nearly everything else goes through United Parcel Service. Both have large facilities within 10 miles of the warehouse. Products that are unusually big or heavy (150 lbs. or more) require special delivery.

2 In suburban Atlanta, three red lights go on

Your order is transmitted to the closest facility that has the products. Amazon's newest, in McDonough, Ga., opened in October and stocks more than a million items. Rows of red lights show which products are ordered. Workers move from bulb to bulb, retrieving an item from the shelf above and pressing a button that resets the light. Computers determine which workers go where.

7 Your order arrives at your doorstep

Voila! One to seven days later, yet another of Amazon's 13 million customers has been served.
—**By Joe Zeff**

"When I started I was one of the fastest pickers here," says John Edwards. "But now that I do other jobs, some people have passed me by."

"Picking" means roaming the aisles of the Seattle distribution center, filling customer orders from shelves packed with titles arranged according to a bewildering strategy called "random stow" that leaves *Toni Morrison: A Womanist Discourse* abutting *Garfield's Extreme Student Planner*. This facility is the smallest of Amazon's nine worldwide distribution centers. But on this December morning, the place is humming with hundreds of pickers pushing around carts piled high with books and other products destined to land under tens of thousands of Christmas trees.

This is how Amazon's other half lives. At least 40% of the work force labors in a distribution center or customer-service center. It's the blue-collar work of the Internet. Neon hair, body piercings and non-Caucasian skin tones are generously represented. And so is the Amazon work ethic. "You have to prove yourself," says Edwards, 30, who came here from a print shop. "But once they notice that you're on time, hardworking and consistent, good things happen," he says.

Sky-high expectations pervade a company that's growing so fast that entire meetings revolve around how to phone-screen the countless job supplicants; recently more than 400 people applied for four openings. The company, like any growing society, has developed a caste system that embitters some in the lower orders. "I hated working there," says an ex-employee. "My bosses were bad managers who just happened to sign on earlier than I did. There was this arrogance, like, 'I'm employee No. 117, and I'm going to be a multimillionaire, so do what I say.'"

Yes, the money. Oh, to be one of the Amazon anointed, those who signed on early and are enjoying multimillion-dollar payouts. Rewards like money make it easy for most Amazonians to embrace the company's hyperyouthful, workaholic Weltanschauung. They go to movie screenings and rave about their fierce broomball rivalry. They throw Friday-night keggers, Valentine's Day parties and masquerade balls. Last fall's Halloween party was so huge that PacMed security guys were checking IDs at the door. WELCOME CAMPUS RECRUITS reads one note scrawled on an elevator whiteboard, summing up the prevailing spirit. AMAZON UBER ALLES! ∎

PHOTOGRAPHS FOR TIME BY DAVID BURNETT—CONTACT

Steve Liss for **TIME**

Americans spent the year worrying more about the corridors of their local schools than the corridors of power in Washington. In the brutal calculus of classroom cliques, everyone seemed to be at risk, outsiders and insiders alike. "Cruelty has consequences," reader Stephen Kroh wrote TIME. "It's not about metal detectors and searches—it's about finally stopping the bullies."

THERE'S A PLACE FOR US: High school outcasts known as the Church Step Dirties hang out in Webster Groves, Mo.

Nation

FLIGHT: Columbine students flee the building to seek shelter

ONE NATION UNDER THE GUN

In Colorado, schoolkids kill schoolkids without reason or mercy, ushering in a year of mass murders and rampages

AMERICANS SPENT MUCH OF the last year of the century in the crosshairs of a gunsight. April was the year's cruelest month, when two high school boys in Colorado staged a brutal, senseless assault on their own classmates. The succeeding months were a calendar of gore. In July, a father in Georgia killed his wife and children, then opened fire at two brokerage offices where he was a day trader, killing five. Later in July, a racist shot up a Jewish center in Los Angeles, then murdered a Filipino-American postman. In September, a gunman invaded a church in Fort Worth, killing four members of a youth group. On Nov. 2, a gunman killed seven in Hawaii; on Nov. 3 another wounded two and killed two in Seattle.

It was the grim slaughter at Colorado's Columbine High School that most dismayed Americans, opening a sad national conversation about what turned two boys' souls into poison, about why smart, privileged kids rot inside. Do we blame the parents, blame the savage music the kids listened to, blame the ease of stockpiling an arsenal, blame the chemistry of cruelty and cliques that has always been a part of high school life but has never been so deadly? Among the many things that did not survive that sad day was the hymn all parents unconsciously sing as they send their children out in the morning, past the headlines, to their schools: It can't happen here. Lord, no, it could never happen here.

By the fall, when the virus of mass murders had spread from coast to coast, the nation was beginning to move beyond denial. Mass murder could—and did—happen all too often in America. Yet though polls showed more Americans favored enacting tougher gun legislation, bitterly partisan Congressmen proved unable to pass such laws. The only major action taken by year's end: schools across the nation clamped down on security, taking extraordinary measures to protect their students.

Yet amid the year's horrors, there was powerful goodness to be found. As Dylan Klebold and Eric Harris prowled Columbine High School in Littleton, Colo., with their guns and bombs, this is what the children did: a boy draped himself over his sister and her friend, so that he would be the one shot. A boy with 10 bullet wounds in his leg picked up an explosive that landed by him and hurled it away from other wounded kids. A girl was asked by the gunman if she believed in God, knowing full well the safe answer. "There is a God," she said quietly, "and you need to follow along God's path." The shooter looked down at her. "There is no God," he said, and he shot her in the head. By the end of that gruesome day, 15 people had died.

Before we inventory the evil we cannot fathom, consider the reflexes at work among these happy, lucky kids, born to a generation that is thought to know nothing about sacrifice. They had no way of knowing what would be asked of them, what they were capable of. Among the kids who died and the ones who were prepared to die were the students who stayed behind to open a door or save a friend or build an escape route or barricade a closet or guide the descending SWAT teams into the darkness.

It can't happen here? Sure it can. It can even happen in Littleton, a town of 35,000 near the dusty-tan foothills of the Rockies, just southwest of Denver. It is a stretched finger of the big city, with aspiring families who don't lock their doors. There's an arch over a hallway in the high school engraved with a motto: THE FINEST KIDS IN AMERICA PASS THROUGH THESE HALLS.

The day the killers chose for their spree, Tuesday, April 20, was Adolf Hitler's birthday. In the handwritten diary of

ATLANTA: TERROR IN THE OFFICE
A day trader kills his family—and five others

TAKE COVER! Above, passersby flee Barton's fire. Right, the killer with wife Leigh Ann, daughter Mychelle and son Matt

The manager and his assistant greeted Mark Barton warmly when he walked into the Atlanta office of All-Tech Investment Group on Thursday, July 29. Barton paused a moment to commiserate with them over the Dow's nearly 200-point slide. They didn't knew that Barton was packing two handguns; that on Tuesday he had murdered his wife, on Wednesday his son and daughter; that he had just been at the building across the street, at another brokerage, Momentum Securities, where he had also started off with small talk about the declining stock market before opening fire with a 9-mm Glock and a .45-cal. Colt, killing four people. At All-Tech, the pleasantries were about to end too.

Five shots rang out from the meeting room, and the manager and his assistant were on the floor, seriously wounded. With his Colt in one hand and his Glock in the other, Barton went on calmly firing. As he left All-Tech, he uttered a single ghoulish aside: "I hope this won't ruin your trading day."

Five people would die at All-Tech. And by dusk, Barton, 44, had turned his guns on himself as police cornered him at a gas station in an Atlanta suburb. By then, America had seen hours of TV images of panic in Atlanta's streets.

In the days that followed, the dead killer's grim story kept unfolding: financial folly, maudlin suicide notes, adultery, brutality, suspected fraud. Moreover, Barton had been a strong suspect in the unsolved 1993 murders of his first wife and her mother. Barton had used his $300,000 insurance payout from those deaths as the grubstake for his failed trading ventures.

one of the suspects, the anniversary, say the police, was clearly marked as a time to "rock 'n' roll." Some members of Harris' and Klebold's clique, tagged in derision the Trench Coat Mafia, had embraced enough Nazi mythology to spook their classmates. They reportedly wore swastikas on black shirts, spoke German in the halls, talked about whom they hated, whom they would like to kill. Harris and Klebold liked to bowl: when Harris made a good shot, he would throw his arm up and declare: *"Heil Hitler!"*

But they were not really dangerous, right? Every school has its rebels, its Goths in black nail polish and lipstick, its stoners and deadbeats. Fellow students described the Mafiosi as discarded, unwanted "stereotype geeks," who, like the jocks and preppies, had their own table in the cafeteria, their group picture in the yearbook with the caption "Who says we're different? Insanity's healthy. Stay alive, stay different, stay crazy."

The Trench Coats' rivalry with the school's élite had been smoldering for months. Some students say even the teachers picked on the Trench Coats, letting the jocks get away with anything because they were the crown princes. One athlete in particular liked to taunt them. "Dirtbag," he'd say, or maybe, "Nice dress." Others called them "faggots," inbreeds, harassing them by throwing rocks and bottles at them from moving cars. Some of the Trench Coats tried to ignore the hazing, but some snarled back. They made a video for class, a tale of kids in trench coats hunting down their enemies with shotguns. The graffiti in the boys' bathroom warned: COLUMBINE WILL EXPLODE ONE DAY. KILL ALL ATHLETES. ALL JOCKS MUST DIE.

It was all out in the open, all the needles and threats, but in a school of nearly 2,000 busy, ambitious kids, that quiet hissing sound was just background noise, drowned out by the the normal sounds of a Tuesday morning. It was Free Cookie Day in the cafeteria, and there were hundreds of students hanging around the tables and waiting in long lines at the 11:30 lunch hour when the sound of gunfire erupted outside. Students saw two boys in trench coats and masks firing at kids; one tossed something up onto the roof of the school, and it exploded in a flash.

Some kids thought it was a senior prank; they had anticipated balloons filled with shaving cream. Then they were screaming and running. One boy could feel the rush of

DYLAN KLEBOLD: "You got the feeling he had low self-esteem," said a friend

a bullet past his head. The kids dove for cover, then began crawling—under furniture, over backpacks, slithering toward the stairs. Bullets clanged as they bounced off metal lockers. Some students tried to run upstairs, to the safety of the library. But smoke was everywhere, the fire alarms had gone off, and the sprinkler system was turning the school into a blinding, misty jungle. So they retreated back downstairs, away from the library, which, by the time the mayhem ended, had become a tomb.

SHERIFF'S DEPUTY NEIL GARDNER, POSTED AT THE school for security, heard the shots and ran toward the cafeteria. When he spotted one gunman, he exchanged fire, then ducked for cover and called for backup. By this time 911 calls were being sent; SWAT cars were on the scene within 20 minutes. But bombs were going off, and the officers had no idea how many shooters there were—or which kids were killers and which were targets. And so the police hunkered down, as the bombs kept exploding all around.

Upstairs in the science wing, science teacher Dick Will herded his charges back to the corner of the room, shut off the lights and started turning over chairs and desks and piling them up against the doors. Business teacher Dave Sanders was in the faculty lounge when he heard the trouble, raced toward the cafeteria and went to war. "He screamed for us to get down and shut up," said freshman Kathy Carlston. "We crawled on the floor and made it to the stairs." When the firing began again, they got up and started to run for a science classroom. Sanders, on the ground, propped himself on his elbows, directing kids to safety as the killers moved in.

Hiding in a science room, Lexis Coffey-Berg saw Sanders running toward him, saw him shot twice in the back. Sanders stumbled into the room, blood streaming from his chest, and collapsed over the desk, knocking out his teeth. A teacher got the paramedics on the phone, and the classroom became a trauma ward. But Sanders did not survive.

Many of the kids who made it out the exits ran into the parking lots. Neighbors arrived with blankets, bandages and gauze. A nurse passing through the area found herself doing triage on a front

ERIC HARRIS: "[He] was always in the garage with the door closed," said a neighbor

L. A.: TERROR AT A JEWISH CENTER
A white supremacist wounds five, kills one

WALK THIS WAY: Above, police lead children to safety; left, Furrow at an Aryan Nations gathering

He always paid the rent and never bothered anybody. Friends say Buford O. ("Neal") Furrow loved children. The heavyset mechanic, a proud white supremacist who was a member of the right wing Aryan Nations group, grew up with guns in the Pacific Northwest, where hunting is a cherished pastime. Jailed after brandishing a knife at a psychiatric hospital, Furrow had been on medication and living at his parents' home since his release on probation in May 1999. Then on Saturday, Aug. 7, he up and left.

Furrow headed for Los Angeles, carrying a rifle, an Israeli-made Uzi, several handguns and a stockpile of ammo. On Aug. 10, in the Granada Hills area of Los Angeles, he saw his target. He walked into the lobby of the North Valley Jewish Community Center carrying the Uzi and opened fire, spraying bullets in a sweeping motion from right to left, leaving a room filled with acrid smoke and more than 70 shells scattered on the floor. By the time he ran out the door moments later, a 68-year-old receptionist, a 16-year-old camp counselor at the day-care center and three children were wounded.

After hijacking a car, Furrow drove to the residential area of Chatsworth and spotted Joseph Ileto, 39, a Filipino-American postman making his rounds. Furrow hit Ileto with a series of three shots, killing him. Almost 24 hours—and an $800 cab ride—later and 275 miles away, in Las Vegas, Furrow calmly turned himself in to federal authorities. He used his newfound notoriety to herald his crime spree as a wake-up call to America to kill Jews.

FORT WORTH: TERROR IN CHURCH

A gunman turns his sights on Christian teenagers

A TIME FOR PRAYER: Members of a Fort Worth Methodist youth group at a service the day after the shootings at Wedgwood Baptist Church

The man who strolled into Wedgwood Baptist Church in Fort Worth, Texas, on Sept. 15 wore jeans and was smoking a cigarette. First Larry Gene Ashbrook, 47, shot Jeff Laster, 36, a seminarian working as a janitor, who survived. His next target was Sydney Browning, 36, the children's choir director, who died. Then Ashbrook shot Shawn Brown, 23, a young man who was staffing a CD sales booth; he also died. In the sanctuary, Ashbrook found a roomful of adolescents: a band was playing a song titled *Alle, Alleluia*. When he was invited by one youth to accept the Lord, Ashbrook moved to the back of the sanctuary, banged a door to get the kids' attention, and started firing randomly, hitting Kim Jones, 23, and several teenagers.

Some of the teens thought the church was staging a skit. It was not. Ashbrook shot and reloaded, shot and reloaded. After he pulled out a small pipe bomb, lit it and rolled it down the aisle—it exploded harmlessly—some kids broke for the doors. Ashbrook strolled to a back pew and shot himself fatally in the temple. In his wake, three adults and four teenagers lay dead.

lawn. The ambulances began shuttling the wounded—the ones who had been able to get out of the building on their own power—to area hospitals.

In the end, the killers did their deadliest work in the school's quietest place. An art teacher, Patti Nielson, was shot; she made it into the library a few steps ahead of them. First she called the police. Then, over the phone, she could be overheard desperately trying to warn the kids. "There's a guy with a gun!" she yelled, bleeding. "Kids, under the table! Kids, stay on the floor!" Craig Scott ducked under a table with his friend Matt Kechter and one of Columbine's few black students, a senior named Isaiah Shoels. And they heard the gunmen come in.

They were laughing, excited. "Who's next?" they said, "Who's ready to die?" The killers went round the room, asking people why they should let them live. "All the jocks stand up," they taunted. "We're going to kill every one of you." Students heard one girl pleading for her life, then a shot and quiet. They approached another girl, cowering under a table, yelled "Peekaboo!" and shot her in the neck. Anyone who cried or moaned was shot again. The murderers were utterly without pity. Survivors said they treated it like a video game.

Craig Scott took off his white baseball hat and hid it. When the killers walked by, they saw Isaiah and called him a "nigger." He pleaded with them not to shoot, just let him go home, he wanted his mom, and they pulled the trigger. Then they shot Matt. Covered in his friends' blood, Craig lay very, very still, praying for courage. "God told me to get out of there," he said. As he got up and started to run, one girl pleaded for help. "She had a chunk of her shoulder blown off with a shotgun," Craig said. "And I helped her get out. She was bleeding all over the place, and her—her bone was showing." They got out of the library, out to an exit, down to the cops, where Craig told them what the shooters looked like, where they were.

It took hours to catalog the carnage. But only on Thursday did officials truly appreciate the level of mayhem the killers had in mind. In the school kitchen, in a duffel bag, they found a sinister parcel containing a propane tank, gasoline can and nails and BBs and glass. The device would have taken dozens of lives in the busy cafeteria.

Before they fired their last two shots into their own heads, the killers fired off some 900 rounds, using two sawed-off shotguns, a 9-mm semiautomatic carbine and a TEC-DC 9 semiautomatic handgun. As the smoke cleared, police discovered more than 30 bombs in all: several pipe bombs in the school and others outside in cars in the parking lot, an arsenal so large that suspicions arose about whether Harris and Klebold could possibly have acted alone. But no evidence of another's complicity surfaced.

The hardest thing about the search for an explanation was the growing fear that there might not be one. There would be lots of talk about the venomous culture that these boys soaked in—but many kids drink those waters without turning into mass murderers. There would be talk of deep family dysfunction, something in their past or their present, but no explanation for something so massively wrong emerged. The killers' parents came to all the Little League and soccer games. They even came to practices.

DYLAN KLEBOLD WAS SAID TO BE THE WEAKER SPIRIT of the two: quiet, reserved, looking for a leader, which he found in Eric Harris when the Harrises moved to Littleton from Plattsburgh, N.Y. Klebold's father Thomas is a former geophysicist who launched a mortgage-management business from his home; his mother Susan worked with blind and disabled kids at the local community college.

Harris' father Wayne was a decorated Air Force pilot. His son's personal website detailed advice on building pipe bombs. "I will rig up explosives all over town," he wrote. "I don't care if I live or die." Klebold and Harris had charmed their way through the legal system once before. Convicted of a felony in 1998 after breaking into a van and stealing about $400 worth of electronic equipment, they cleared their records by participating in community-service programs and an anger-management seminar.

Yet the police disclosed that the handwritten diary they had found was drenched in Nazi-philia: phrases in German punctuating a year's worth of meticulous plan-

ning for the attack on Hitler's 110th birthday. There were also annotated maps of the school showing the best places to hide and where and when the most students gathered. Yet however much the duo hated the school's jocks, the killings were, in the end, blindly indiscriminate. They shot at the math whiz and the actress, the wrestler, the debater, jocks, brains, band members, freshmen, seniors. They shot at the head football coach; they shot at the science teacher.

By the time the flowers piled up in the soft spring snow in the school parking lot, the recriminations were well under way. How could parents not know their garage was a bombmaking factory? How could a school not know the hatred in its halls was more than routine teenage alienation? Why had the SWAT team members been so cautious when people were trapped and bleeding to death? There were no answers, only memorials. On a hill outside Littleton, 15 crosses were planted, 13 for the victims and two, set apart, for their killers. Later those two crosses were cut down by the father of one of the slain students.

By then, other crosses had been erected, in other towns across America: in Atlanta, in Los Angeles, in Fort Worth. The uneasiness, the groping for explanations, the fear and the shame ranged far beyond Littleton's hills. And the question Americans asked themselves was no longer: Can it happen here? It was: What are we going to do about it? ■

ELEGY: Amber Johnson, front, writes a note for the shooting victims at a memorial site in Clement Park in Littleton

THE
WHITE HOUSE MARATHON

On your mark, get set, go—through scores of speeches, hundreds of plane flights, thousands of handshakes and millions of dollars—to win the Oval Office

GOTTA RUN! Owner must go by Jan. '01, but the time to act is now! Great central D.C. location, superb house staff and curb appeal to die for. Like fixer-uppers? I could use a good cleaning.

AND THEY'RE OFF! EIGHTEEN months before the November 2000 election, a passel of hopefuls was already running hard to take up residence in the White House. All eyes were fixed on the early tests: the New Hampshire primary on Feb. 1, 2000 and the parties' staggered Iowa caucuses. In today's warp-speed political world, 11 Republicans announced their candidacy during 1999—and by December five of them had dropped out.

BRADLEY: He sandbagged Gore

GORE: "Hey, Bill, I got game too!"

The Democrats had a surprise as well: Vice President Al Gore, long billed a shoo-in for their nomination, faced a strong challenge from former New Jersey Senator Bill Bradley. The Reform Party was playing its usual role, a not-ready-for-prime-time sideshow. Angling to shrug off the yoke of founder Ross Perot, party members staged a free-for-all involving a former wrestler (Minnesota Governor Jesse Ventura), a G.O.P. refusenik (Pat Buchanan) and a playboy billionaire (self-infatuated developer Donald Trump).

REPUBLICAN RUMBLE. For much of the year, the G.O.P. race resembled *Snow White and the Dwindling Dwarfs*. In June Texas Governor George W. Bush, eldest son of ex-President George Herbert Walker Bush, came roaring out of Austin with so much money and momentum behind him that it seemed the campaign was over before it began. His secret: while his parents quietly lobbied their 5,000 closest friends, Michigan Governor John Engler was building a Bush power base among the nation's G.O.P. Governors, the only Republicans who got away with their shirts in the 1998 elec-

tions. And all the while, Prince George stayed in Texas: he went nowhere near Iowa or New Hampshire, gave few big speeches and cruised to a crushing re-election victory. Then, in a pre-emptive fiscal strike, he announced on June 30 that his campaign had amassed a mighty war chest of $36 million; by November it had grown to $50 million.

Bush's push was so potent that it scared several G.O.P. candidates off the track before the race had really begun. Former Vice President Dan Quayle, House budget expert John Kasich and onetime Secretary of Education Lamar Alexander had all called it quits by August. And on Oct. 20, Elizabeth Dole, longtime Washington power player and wife of the 1996 G.O.P. nominee, Bob Dole, withdrew from the race she had entered only seven months before. Said Dole, who had been considered one of Bush's strongest challengers: "Money is the bottom line." Her withdrawal—and Pat Buchanan's bolting to the Reform Party—left Bush facing a batch of overmatched, underfunded contenders: conservative columnist Alan Keyes, right-wing pro-lifer Gary Bauer, little-known Senator Orrin Hatch of Utah and third-time candidate Steve Forbes. The wealthy magazine publisher was still pitching his flat-tax proposal but was newly outspoken in his advocacy of values issues close to conservative Christian hearts.

While his opponents hewed to the right, Bush took dead aim on the middle of the road, trumpeting a theme of "compassionate conservatism" and stressing the social issues that resonated with voters: education, health care, child care. In October he gave his own

MC CAIN: Never a loss for words

BUSH: The G.O.P.'s crown prince

party a carefully calibrated thwack, saying the G.O.P. was too often indifferent to the "human problems that persist in the shadow of affluence." He thus got credit for being caring and optimistic while distancing himself from congressional Republicans and from Washington.

But by this time Bush was in a real race. In late April, 62-year-old former Navy pilot and Vietnam War hero Senator John McCain of Arizona, then considering a run, found traction when he blasted Bill Clinton's Kosovo policy. While

SECOND ACT FOR A THIRD PARTY

Already divided, the Reform crowd gets ditzier

With its access to state ballots and $12.6 million in federal matching funds, the Reform Party nomination is a real prize. But the party is torn between founder Ross Perot and its highest-ranking elected official, Minnesota Governor Jesse Ventura. At its convention, Ventura's man, Jack Gargan, a retired financial consultant, was elected chairman. Here's the cast of Reform characters:

JESSE VENTURA
The erstwhile pro wrestler didn't show up at the party's summer convention; instead, he let down its delegates by declaring via long distance that he would not pursue its nomination for President. But Ventura wanted to keep the nod from going to either Ross Perot or Pat Buchanan. In September he held a summit meeting in Atlantic City, N.J., with Donald Trump, whom he admires and would clearly favor over Buchanan.

PAT BUCHANAN
In October the right-wing commentator and perennial candidate made good on a threat to bolt the G.O.P. to seek the Reform Party nod. He also released a book, *A Republic, Not an Empire,* that caused an outcry with its assertion

that America should not have opposed Hitler in World War II. Once again, Buchanan's message centered on his nationalist and anti-free-trade arguments and his anti-Washington populism.

DONALD TRUMP
The twice-divorced billionaire real estate mogul was exploring a Reform candidacy centered on a one-time soak-the-rich tax hike; he was opposed to affirmative action but was pro-choice. Would anyone vote for the king of broads and blackjack, prenups and palaces? "The guy who gets $50 in chips and a ticket for the all-you-can-eat buffet and takes the missus to the Trump Taj Mahal loves me," the Donald declared.

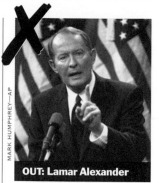

OUT: Lamar Alexander

other Republicans temporized, McCain called for weighing the use of ground troops and criticized Clinton for "trying to avoid war while waging one." In September, McCain threw his hat in the ring and began to throw a scare into Bush.

The maverick Senator was known to most Americans mainly for his unsuccessful efforts to reform the nation's campaign-finance laws and curb pork-barrel spending, stands that infuriated his colleagues. But his numbers soared as more voters became aware of his heroic past: the son and grandson of four-star Navy admirals, he had been a prisoner in the

In the first post-Brylcreem race for the White

"Hanoi Hilton" for 5½ years after his fighter plane was shot down. By October he was even with Bush in polls of New Hampshire voters; by December he was leading the Texan.

Now Bush and McCain began to face serious scrutiny. Early on, Bush had fought off persistent rumors of drug use in his youth by refusing to take questions on the subject, hiding behind the well-crafted phrase, "When I was young and irresponsible, I was young and irresponsible." A more serious charge persisted: Bush was an intellectual lightweight—"all hat and no cattle," in the local argot. In Austin he was known as a confident, crisp decision maker. But on the national stage, a competing image had appeared—that of a cautious, staff-dependent candidate, likable but lacking gravitas, who often sounded out of his depth on serious policy issues, especially in foreign affairs. When a Boston TV reporter ambushed him with a tough pop quiz on world leaders, Bush flunked, failing to name the heads of four countries. He fought his party-boy image with a well-received address on foreign policy at the Ronald Reagan Library in California, but the tag stuck.

As for McCain, he was accused of having an unpredictable, hair-trigger temper, most notably in a November editorial in his hometown paper, the Arizona *Republic,* which painted him as a bully, sarcastic and insulting. McCain countered the charge by releasing a complete medical history, which quieted his critics for the time being.

One Navy prince, one political prince, both rebel cutups with frat-house charm—McCain and Bush were alike, yet very different men. If Bush was defined by his friends, McCain was known by the enemies he had dared to make. Whereas Bush spent his early years at play, with a father who made life easy, McCain spent his as a prisoner of war, with a father tough enough to order the

OUT: Dan Quayle

bombing of the city where his son was held captive. Bush, all lightness of being, struggled to be viewed as serious enough for the job; McCain, all coiled conviction, was so intense he had to struggle to be seen as normal. One hoped to give his party a heart, the other a conscience.

DEMOCRATIC DUEL. If the Republicans began the presidential marathon with too many candidates, the Democrats had too few: Al Gore stood alone, ready for his coronation. But his bandwagon ran into trouble when three-time Senator Bill Bradley, retired since 1996, began a well-staged run for the nomination.

Bradley was the uncola, the all-natural candidate. He still drove a battered '84 Oldsmobile, and he didn't mall-test his ideas. He scolded anyone who pressed him on an issue he hadn't thought through. He wouldn't go negative; for that matter, he barely went positive. This anti-Clinton slicked

seat drivers, he squandered huge leads in two key categories: money and sheer inevitability.

Finally, Gore got the message. On Sept. 29 he fired his pollster, slashed his staff, declared himself the underdog and moved his headquarters from Washington to Nashville, Tenn. Reinventing himself, he donned casual duds and traded in elaborately staged campaign events for passionate one-on-ones with voters, the better to showcase his mastery of a wide range of the issues. In October he won the critical endorsement of the American Federation of Labor, and his poll numbers began to stabilize against Bradley's. The two deep thinkers promised to give Democrats a bracing

OUT: Elizabeth Dole

House, the candidates hankered for authenticity and polished their flaws like medals

himself up for no man. The former basketball star for a legendary New York Knicks team boasted high-mindedness, dogged integrity and a seeming indifference to the game of politics—qualities tailor-made for a post-Clinton age.

His foe had just the opposite problem: famously starchy, Gore was stuck with the stench of Clinton and had too much Brylcreem in his presentation. Even as Bradley began cutting into his lead, the Vice President was high on endorsements but low on energy. Orbited by a virtual asteroid belt of pollsters, message advisers and back-

ALL EARS: Moynihan wannabes heed the siren call of office

contest of ideas right down to the finish line. And may the least-slick candidate win!

For if there was a single element that united all the candidates in the long slog to the White House, it was their quest to wield the sword of authenticity. The focus on Bush's intellect and McCain's temper, on Bradley's old car and Gore's new clothes, reflected the voters' mandate that candidates scrap the imagemongers and get real. In America's evolving anti-façade campaign, would-be Presidents were polishing their flaws like medals. ■

IN NEW YORK, THE SOUND AND THE FURY
Enough, already! Voters cower as Rudy and Hillary rev up

And you thought the race for the White House went on too long? In New York State, voters were complaining of campaign overload 16 months before they would go to the polls to replace departing Senator Patrick Moynihan. Reason: the fight for his seat was shaping up as a battle between two magnets for controversy—New York City Mayor Rudolph Giuliani and the First Lady of the land, Hillary Rodham Clinton.

Talk of a Hillary run began as a low buzz in January and ended the year as a round-the-clock media roar, after she concluded months of hedging in late November and declared she would seek the seat. The contrast between the pair's public personas was delicious—Republican Giuliani, the pugnacious former prosecutor who cleaned up the New York City streets; Democrat Hillary, the committed liberal and betrayed wife so long scrutinized by another prosecutor.

Early on, Hillary seemed to have the edge. Among the Democrats' core constituencies—Manhattan

liberals, women, unions and minorities—it seemed she would bury Giuliani. Yet even as she energized Democrats, she united New York's fractious Republicans. And Giuliani's brutally efficient success in reducing crime, paring welfare rolls and fighting smut in his city had endeared him to middle-class whites outside Manhattan, while his pro-choice moderation on social issues made him palatable to soccer moms.

By December, Hillary had lost serious ground in voter polls, aggravated by a blunder during a trip to the Middle East: she stood by silently while Suha Arafat, the wife of the Palestinian leader, accused Israel of using cancer-causing poison gas on Palestinian women and children. The gaffe tarnished her image in the Jewish community, a group whose support she needed. Two facts were clear: New York voters were in for a long haul—and the Empire State's next Senator would turn out to be the candidate who proved most surefooted in traversing its treacherous electoral landscape.

GIVING UP THE SHIP?

Sinking feeling: Critics howl as Uncle Sam surrenders its control of the Panama Canal

PANAMA HAS ALWAYS BEEN A PLACE WHERE STRANGE truth gives fiction a run for its money. In his 1996 novel *The Tailor of Panama,* John LeCarré imagines a Cockney living in Panama City who tricks money out of British intelligence by stitching up a plot involving Asians' taking over the Panama Canal. In real-life Panama in 1999, the story was no less peculiar: a new President took office amid charges that the government had switched control of the canal to a company allegedly controlled by the Chinese People's Liberation Army. The canal handover—the U.S. passed the waterway over to Panama at noon on Dec. 31—unleashed political separation anxiety in the U.S. and everything from panic to greed in Panama. LeCarré must be amused.

The furor came at a time when Panama is trying to reinvent itself. While only 7% of the country's economy is dependent on the canal, nearly 100% of its self-image is wrapped up in the belief that it serves as one of the world's most important trade links. More ambitious Panamanians (and the country's well-educated middle class is full of them) talk of becoming the Singapore of Latin America. Doing that means making the post-handover canal as profitable as possible.

The burden of reinvention fell on the shoulders of Mireya Moscoso, 53, after an election in which the widow of one Panamanian president defeated the son of another. Moscoso, widow of the three-time populist President Arnulfo Arias, won nearly 45% of the vote in May, while Martin Torrijos, son of the late dictator General Omar Torrijos, took nearly 38%. Moscoso's challenge is to turn a world-class location into a world-class country, technologically literate and oriented to the future.

The handover spooked conservative Americans because the Panamanians were working assiduously to make the canal—which has always been run on a nonprofit basis—into a cash cow. It is not a new complaint. In 1978, when President Jimmy Carter sold the handover treaty to Congress, there was much whining about turning the canal into little more than an expensive toll road. The lat-

est version of this anxiety added a national security tweak: fear of China. In 1997, the Panamanian government finalized a rich deal with Hutchison Whampoa Ltd., based in Hong Kong, to run two ports near the entrances to the canal. U.S.-owned Bechtel lost out to Hutchison under a questionable bidding process.

American officials at the time complained that the Bake-Off was, at the least, "unorthodox." The issue was rekindled in August when Senate majority leader Trent Lott complained that the U.S. had "given the farm away without a shot being fired." In particular, said Lott, the deal meant "U.S. naval ships will be at the mercy of Chinese-controlled pilots and could even be denied passage by Hutchison," which he called "an arm of the People's Liberation Army."

Few observers agreed with the majority leader's view that Hutchison is an arm of the P.L.A. The publicly held firm manages 19 ports in Asia, Europe and the Americas; shipping experts consider it among the world's finest. And, said Joseph Cornelison, the commission's deputy administrator, "we'll control the timing of ships going in and out of Hutchison's ports." Moreover, under the treaty, U.S. Navy

KEVIN JENKINS—IPOL

How It Works

The average ship requires 8 to 10 hours to move through the Canal, which is 50 miles (80 km) long. Three sets of locks lift ships from one ocean into Gatun Lake and then lower them into the other ocean. The Canal collects $650 million annually in revenues, an average of $34,000 in tolls per ship. More than 9,000 Panamanians are employed

Why It Matters

ESSENTIAL TRADE ROUTE More than 825,000 vessels have passed through the Canal since it opened in 1914. Cargo ships travelling from the U.S. east coast to Japan save 3,000 miles (4,800 km) by not having to go around South America. A 1977 treaty transfers the Canal to Panama on Dec. 31, 1999

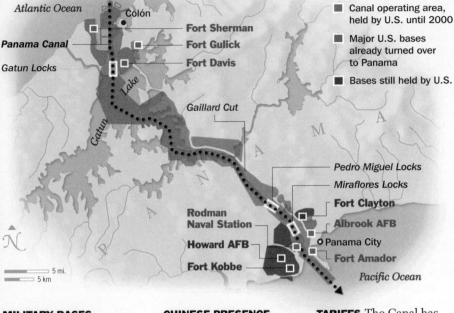

Atlantic Ocean
Colón
Fort Sherman
Panama Canal
Fort Gulick
Gatun Locks
Fort Davis
Gatun Lake
Gaillard Cut

■ Canal operating area, held by U.S. until 2000
■ Major U.S. bases already turned over to Panama
■ Bases still held by U.S.

Pedro Miguel Locks
Miraflores Locks
Fort Clayton
Rodman Naval Station
Albrook AFB
Howard AFB
Panama City
Fort Kobbe
Fort Amador
Pacific Ocean

5 mi.
5 km

MILITARY BASES
U.S. Southern Command was based here. Besides defending the Canal, troops were very involved in counter-drug operations that have now moved elsewhere

CHINESE PRESENCE
In 1997 a Hong Kong company was awarded a 25-year contract to run terminals at both ends. Republicans claim the company is involved with the Chinese government

TARIFFS The Canal has been run as a nonprofit utility, but that will change. Some worry that Panama could suddenly raise tariffs or keep profits and not reinvest for needed improvements

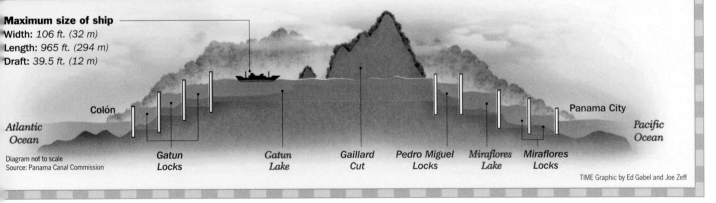

Maximum size of ship
Width: *106 ft. (32 m)*
Length: *965 ft. (294 m)*
Draft: *39.5 ft. (12 m)*

Atlantic Ocean
Colón
Gatun Locks
Gatun Lake
Gaillard Cut
Pedro Miguel Locks
Miraflores Lake
Miraflores Locks
Panama City
Pacific Ocean

Diagram not to scale
Source: Panama Canal Commission

TIME Graphic by Ed Gabel and Joe Zeff

ships will keep their privilege of cutting to the front of the line of vessels waiting to use the canal. Alarmists countered by pointing out that the treaty allows the U.S. to intervene militarily—but only if the canal's neutrality is menaced. Critics of the plan included presidential candidates Gary Bauer, Pat Buchanan and John McCain.

President-elect Moscoso took office with enough troubles on her desk. She lacked a legislative majority, and any concession allowing the U.S. military back into Panama would be unpopular. Moscoso picked up her political acu-

men from her late husband, Arias, though a 46-year age gap separated her from the former President. His career provides a sobering lesson. Arias was elected three times, and each time the army deposed him. Diplomats in Panama say Moscoso knows she must tread cautiously if she is to avoid his fate. She vowed she would keep politics out of the handover, entrusting the canal's operations to the autonomous Panama Canal Authority. Moscoso expects Washington to do the same, leaving rumbles of Chinese conspiracies to the thriller writers. ■

Will the Flames of Waco Ever Die?

Revelations force the Attorney General to confront a tragic encounter—again

ONCE IT WAS EASY TO PASS over a story like David Thibodeau's. He is one of only nine people to survive the burning of David Koresh's Branch Davidian compound in Waco, Texas, on April 19, 1993. And he says he saw a shiny thing embedded in a wall of the compound chapel that day, where he took refuge with fellow believers during a lull between government tear-gas assaults. In the

RENO: Playing defense

calm, Thibodeau studied the thing. "It was the size of a Coke can," he says. "Silver, stainless steel in color. There were three fins on the back. It was some kind of projectile." Before he could look more closely, however, the screech of tanks started up again. Chaos ensued. Then fire.

Thibodeau's tale of the wayward rocket is one of many that in 1999 rekindled conspiracy theories that the government had started the fires that killed some 80 men, women and children. Other newly identified flying objects turned this piece of rural Texas into Attorney General Janet Reno's Area 51, a place full of things she did not know existed.

A humiliated Reno admitted in late August that it appeared the FBI had fired pyrotechnic military tear-gas rounds during the showdown with the Branch Davidians. For years, she and the bureau had denied that such "hot" devices had been used. Reno insisted—and most evidence indicates—the grenades were launched too early in the day and had landed too far away to cause the fires. But, Reno added, "I did not want those [hot grenades] used. I asked for and received assurances that [any used] were not incendiary." She later named former Missouri Senator John Danforth to head a new probe of a controversy she thought she had put behind her.

Reno denied that she was furious at the FBI and its director, Louis Freeh. Yet days later, she sent U.S. marshals into FBI headquarters in the Hoover building to "take custody of" (not "seize," she and

the FBI insisted) evidence that the bureau's crack Hostage Rescue Team had fired such grenades during the siege.

With the can of worms open, more charges followed. Filmmaker Michael McNulty, a dogged FBI critic, purportedly had footage of an agency helicopter opening fire on the Davidians; the FBI has always claimed that its agents never shot at the cultists. More trouble for Reno and the FBI may still lie undetected in their files. James B. Francis, head of the élite Texas Rangers (regional rivals of the FBI), charges that Army Delta Force units may have taken part in the siege, a violation of the law. The Pentagon conceded that three Army personnel were in Waco on April 19, but only as observers and advisers.

Janet Reno ordered U.S. marshals into FBI headquarters to "take custody of"—not "seize"—evidence

FBI and Justice officials, buttressed by forensic evidence and transcripts of bugged conversations among the Davidians, remain convinced that cult members ignited the fires that consumed them. Still, 1999's admissions made it seem that Agent Mulder of TV's *X-Files* might be right: the truth is out there. But Janet Reno, Justice and the FBI, in bureau parlance, couldn't find a pie in a bakery. ∎

THE COMPOUND: The FBI claims its agents did not set the fire that engulfed David Koresh's camp, but it has lost its credibility. Inset, a military round fired at Waco

PAUL JOSEPH BROWN—SEATTLE POST INTELLIGENCER

POINT BLANK: A policeman fires rubber bullets at the height of the riots, when violent anarchists took over the streets

Trading Punches: The Battle in Seattle

Raging against the machine, a motley crew of protesters sabotages trade talks

THE BUREAUCRATS MAY NOT HAVE ACCOMPLISHED ALL that much at the late-fall meeting of the World Trade Organization in Seattle. The chaos that surrounded them did. In this year of triumphant capitalism, of planetary cash flows and a priapic Dow, all the second thoughts and outright furies about the global economy collected on the streets of Seattle and crashed through the windows of NikeTown. After two days of uproar scented with tear gas and pepper spray, Americans may finally confront the issues surrounding free trade and its costs.

The WTO delegates had come to Seattle to draw up an agenda for a new round of global-trade talks, which are scheduled to last about three years and take up issues like European farm subsidies—of huge importance to U.S. and Canadian agricultural exporters. But they ran into a coalition of protesters that cut across ideologies: environmentalists, labor unionists, isolationist Buchananites, opponents of child labor, proponents of Tibetan freedom, antiglobalists, anarchists, even old-time Pacific Northwest Wobblies.

The protests began on Tuesday, Nov. 30, the conference's opening day. As 25,000 largely peaceful marchers headed from a union-backed rally into downtown, they met with many thousands of other demonstrators, who were mainly taking part in nonviolent sit-ins that blocked

traffic. Things got serious when scattered groups of self-described Black Block anarchists, wearing all-black outfits with handkerchiefs or hoods covering their faces, started to smash windows and trash businesses, targeting companies such as the Gap and Nike that have been accused of using low-wage or child labor to produce goods.

As the violence heated up, police used rubber bullets, tear gas and pepper spray against the rioters. With the streets in chaos and frustrated delegates confined to their hotels, a stunned Mayor Paul Schell imposed a curfew and a no-protest order on downtown and asked Washington Governor Gary Locke to send in the National Guard.

Police restored order by arresting about 500 demonstrators on Wednesday, the day Bill Clinton arrived. The President used the protests as a chance to argue in an interview for the WTO to develop "core" standards for wages, working conditions and other labor issues—infuriating delegates from developing nations. By late Friday night, negotiations on the agenda for the new round of talks collapsed, and the delegates departed Seattle empty-handed. Their opponents departed full of hope: they had driven trade issues from inside Washington's Beltway and onto America's streets. And Seattle police chief Norm Stamper departed his office. Somebody had to be the scapegoat. ∎

Images

A SPIRE'S ATTIRE
Take our word for it: Bill Clinton is in the chopper at right, returning from an engagement. What we really want you to look at in this picture is the Washington Monument, which is undergoing an 18-month, $9.4 million renovation. Post-modern architect Michael Graves designed a luminous "skin" of translucent blue polyester mesh to hide the scaffolding around the 555-ft.-high obelisk. And—presto!—the spire became a numinous 21st century version of itself, resulting in pleas that the shroud be left in position.

Tragedy in Texas

Texas A&M commands a loyalty among its students and alumni that approaches fanaticism. Its most enduring tradition is a 90-year-old rite: the building and torching of a massive bonfire on the eve of the annual football game with arch-rival University of Texas. Erecting it demands weeks of around-the clock labor by 5,000 student volunteers and the felling of 5,000 oaks. On Nov. 18, at 2:28 a.m., as scores of students swarmed over it, the 44-ft.-tall tower buckled, then toppled, as the kids scrambled for safety. The lucky ones escaped. The rest were entombed in a mess of logs and wires. (Witnesses thought the center pole—two thick pine trunks bound together and pounded 10 ft. into the earth—had snapped.) Frantic rescuers found 12 dead and 28 injured, leaving a heart-breaking pile of questions: Were sufficient precautions taken? Was the students' supervision adequate? And is any ceremony worth such risk?

PAT SULLIVAN—AP/WIDE WORLD

GRIM TASK: Rescue workers retrieve a body in Texas

STEPHEN CHERNIN—AP/WIDE WORLD

THE 'BURBS: The new Clinton digs

The Other White House

Be it ever so humble … it's now perhaps the most famous private residence in America. In September, anticipating the First Lady's run for election as a Senator from New York State, Bill and Hillary Rodham Clinton paid $1.7 million for a white colonial house on a private cul-de-sac in the upscale Westchester community of Chappaqua. The small suburban town is located on the eastern bank of the Hudson River; many of its residents commute to work in Manhattan.

Now, Meet Newt's Monica

Speaking of those who live in glass houses: former Speaker of the House and Clinton critic Newt Gingrich, 56, found himself in an ironic fix in 1999. Rumors were flying that he had been romantically linked with Callista Bisek, 33, a staff member on the House Agriculture Committee, well before his July filing for divorce from his second wife Marianne. In August Marianne's lawyers were granted the right to take a videotaped deposition from Bisek as part of the divorce proceedings. A scandal-saturated nation tuned out Newt's nightmare, even when his lawyer called a gift he had given Callista "not even a really nice ring."

Finally, the Scandal Ends

Every poll confirmed that Americans had reached a rough consensus concerning President Bill Clinton's behavior in the Monica Lewinsky affair: he was guilty of adultery and deceit, but these private failings did not warrant his removal from office. And every poll confirmed that Americans would rather forget the entire squalid

RUSSELL TURIAK—STAR MAGAZINE

STEPPING OUT: Gingrich and Bisek

mess than recall it. But for the record: on Jan. 7, the U.S. Senate, with Chief Justice of the United States William Rehnquist presiding, convened in the impeachment trial of William Jefferson Clinton. After five weeks of testimony, the Senate voted on the two articles of impeachment. The final tallies: 45-55 to convict on the count of perjury, 50-50 on the count of obstruction of justice—far below the two-thirds majority required to remove a President from office.

People

Refugee from the '70s

The 52-year-old guerrilla lived with her husband the doctor in a $264,000 five-bedroom, four-bath home in St. Paul, Minn., surrounded by well-to-do neighbors. She grew hostas and geraniums and ran a mean marathon. Though she may have once consorted with bank robbers and bombmakers as a member of the '70s radical-fringe group the Symbionese Liberation Army, the soccer mom of three girls was now a gun-control advocate who found time to narrate Christmas pageants, feed the homeless and read to the blind. In this life and on the local stage, where she often appeared, she was known as Sara Jane Olson— her maiden name, she said. But in June, FBI agents who called her Kathleen Ann Soliah arrested her on 24-year-old charges involving allegedly

SYGMA

NABBED: Soliah

planting pipe bombs under police cars and "unlawful flight to avoid prosecution." The case broke after it was featured on the TV show *America's Most Wanted*. Her case will be tried in 2000.

HEAR YE: The Chief Justice presides as House Judiciary Committee members prosecute the President in the Senate

Peter Sanders

A spin of the globe revealed a world beset by troubles in '99: rookie nuclear nations India and Pakistan skirmished in Kashmir, earthquakes rocked Turkey and Taiwan. But there was good news as well: the NATO allies stood up for human rights in Kosovo, the U.N. endorsed East Timor's declaration of independence, and a bipartisan government assumed power in Northern Ireland.

PILGRIMS: Islam's enormous growth forced clerics in Mecca to enlarge the religion's most sacred shrine, the Holy Mosque.

World

A LAND OF EXILES

The NATO allies stop Slobodan Milosevic's brutal rape of Kosovo—but the price is steep

FALSE DAWN:
Kosovar refugees, after a journey by foot, gather near the border of Macedonia

SLOBODAN MILOSEVIC IS THE most disruptive dictator to haunt Europe since the fall of the Berlin Wall. He is a blood-drenched bully: patron of "ethnic cleansing," he bears responsibility for the extermination of 250,000 in Bosnia and Croatia, for the European revival of concentration camps and massacres, for the displacement of millions of residents of the troubled region. And he is a poor leader. He failed to hold together the former Yugoslavia, and he failed to build in its place his dream of a "Greater Serbia." He bears the responsibility for the impoverishment and ostracism of his country.

In 1999 Milosevic inflicted new sorrows on the peoples of the Balkans. Defying an ultimatum by the North Atlantic Treaty Organization, he continued his aggression against the Kosovars, the ethnic Albanian Muslims of Yugoslavia's rebellious Kosovo province. With its credibility on the line, NATO—on the eve of celebrating its 50th anniversary—launched an air attack against Yugoslavia. Milosevic's response was both brutally cruel and strategically brilliant: he used the attack to intensify his assault on the Kosovars, sending hundreds of thousands of them into exile. The exodus flooded neighboring states, creating a crisis that threatened the stability of the region. After 72 days of NATO's nonstop bombing, Milosevic finally caved and agreed to a peace deal. But the damage he had wrought would take years, perhaps decades, to mend.

Kosovo has a complicated genealogy: it is populated mostly by Albanians, but for 600 years it has been a lantern of Serbian passion. Serbs venerate the land because it is home to several important monasteries, and in 1389 their ancestors lost a decisive battle with the Ottoman Empire there, initiating 500 years of Turkish rule. The day of the battle is a national holiday. One of Milosevic's early goals when he came to power in 1989 was to tighten his control over Kosovo. In 1989 he revoked the province's self-government—which it had enjoyed since

CRISIS IN KOSOVO

A KOSOVO PRIMER

■ BACKGROUND TO THE WAR

Yugoslavia, dominated by Serbs, revoked the autonomy of its Kosovo province, where most inhabitants are ethnic Albanian Muslims, in 1989. Hostilities heated up in 1998, as the rebel Kosovo Liberation Army grew in numbers and power. Serbs killed thousands of Kosovars and uprooted tens of thousands more, threatening European security by inflaming passions and creating refugee crises in neighboring Albania, Macedonia and Montenegro.

■ WHAT THEY FOUGHT FOR

MILOSEVIC To keep Kosovo part of Yugoslavia, under Serbian control, and to stop any occupation of the region by NATO forces.

KOSOVARS An immediate cessation of hostilities and atrocities by the Serbs, followed without delay by full independence.

U.S. and NATO For Milosevic to sign a pact that would give Kosovo eventual autonomy, one enforced by NATO troops on the ground.

■ THE REGION

AREA 4,203 sq. mi. (10,887 sq km)—about 60 Kosovos could fit inside Texas.

POPULATION Almost 2 million: 90% ethnic Albanian; 10% Serbian.

■ HISTORY

1389 Ottoman Turks defeat Serb-led armies in Kosovo. Most Serbs then migrate north, but they still consider the region their ancestral homeland.

1929 Kosovo becomes part of the kingdom of Yugoslavia, which, after World War II, becomes a communist republic.

1974 A new constitution gives Kosovo political and economic autonomy.

1989 Rallying Kosovo's Serbian minority, Slobodan Milosevic strips the province of its autonomy.

1992 Kosovo's ethnic Albanians vote to secede from Yugoslavia, as other non-Serbian regions have done. Milosevic stops them with armed force.

1998 Ethnic Albanian guerrilla forces in the Kosovo Liberation Army struggle against Milosevic's forces.

■ ETHNIC PROFILE

Kosovo was the last major non-Serbian ethnic enclave still remaining in Yugoslavia.

■ Serbian
■ Albanian
■ Macedonian
■ Montenegrin
■ Muslim
■ Others

1974—and instead demanded that local Albanians follow orders from Belgrade. Every year the noose got tighter. By 1998 Kosovo was home to a nascent guerrilla movement led by the Kosovo Liberation Army. Occupying Serbs became targets. On Feb. 28, 1998, an Albanian hit squad killed two Serbian policemen working in Kosovo. Milosevic unleashed his security police and paramilitary units in a pitiless reprisal that left 300 dead and 65,000 homeless.

U.S. diplomat Richard Holbrooke, the architect of the 1995 Dayton peace accords that finally brought calm to Bosnia and Herzegovina, worked out a deal with Milosevic to stop the suffering. But it began to collapse almost immediately, and the killings in Kosovo continued. The K.L.A. kept growing in power, killing one or two Serbian police a week—enough to infuriate Milosevic and increase the pressure for reprisals.

On Jan. 15, 1999, Serbian security police killed 45 ethnic Albanian civilians outside the town of Racak. The NATO allies were furious; determined to stop Milosevic before he could devastate yet another ethnic group, they demanded that the Serbs and Kosovars agree to a three-year autonomy plan for Kosovo. After weeks of talks in France, the Kosovar Albanians signed the agreement on March 18. But Milosevic refused, saying he would never allow alien soldiers onto the sacred soil of Kosovo. The allies issued yet another ultimatum: Milosevic must sign or face NATO action, and Bill Clinton and the Pentagon began preparing the U.S. war machine for battle. Clinton was strongly backed by British Prime Minister Tony Blair but received only hesitant approval from some other NATO members, including Italy and Greece.

A last-ditch visit by Holbrooke failed to sway Milosevic. "You can bomb us if you wish," he told the U.S. diplomat on Monday, March 23. Some 36 hours later, NATO obliged. Operation Allied Force sent more than 400 planes from 12 alliance nations against Serbian targets in all three provinces of Yugoslavia: Serbia, Montenegro and Kosovo. The aftershocks of the bombing rattled the globe. U.S. embassies from Moscow to Paris were besieged by furious Serbs, and neighboring states from Albania to Macedonia were convulsed by the prospect of spillover violence. Russian President Boris Yeltsin, whose people share deep ethnic and religious ties with the Serbs, rebuked Bill Clinton in a lengthy phone call.

In the first weeks of the war, Milosevic seemed to be winning, at least by his peculiar calculus. NATO had hoped the bombing would cause him to back down quickly. Instead, he stood firm, ceding the skies to the allies, letting the bombs and missiles rain down while barely activating his air defenses. Meanwhile, on the ground, his army pushed the Albanian Kosovars out of the country and launched a murderous offensive against the K.L.A.

In Pristina, the capital of Kosovo, black-masked Serbian police dragged Albanians out of their homes, force-marched them to a railroad station and packed thousands into locked trains bound for Macedonia. Hundreds of thousands of ethnic Albanians desperately fled their homes, traversing miles of winding mountain roads on foot, by tractor or atop mules. After the first 10 days of bombing, according to the U.N., more than 300,000 refugees had crossed into neighboring Albania, Macedonia and Montenegro. And the numbers kept growing; after the war, the U.N. estimated at least 850,000 refugees had fled the province.

What the refugees left behind was a Serbian spasm of looting, terror and executions; what they encountered on the other side of the frontier was a teeming mess of poverty, hunger and disease. At the Montenegro border, a column of refugees awaiting entry extended in an unbroken line of misery for 20 miles. At one point Macedonia closed its border, while thousands of Kosovars waited to get in. In Montenegro's Rozaje, refugees drifted through the streets, hungry and shell-shocked; some would come across small obstacles and simply stop and weep.

BOMBS AWAY: On April 2, in the war's second week, NATO bombs set an Interior Ministry building in Belgrade afire

Milosevic had succeeded in foisting a barbarous humanitarian crisis upon his neighbors and the European continent. The sight of tens of thousands of dazed, shuddering refugees fleeing for their lives into the region's poorest, least stable states set off shock waves in the West.

SUDDENLY, THE WONDER WEAPONS OF AIR POWER looked futile against primitive paramilitary gangs with guns. The long-threatened bombing campaign was not only failing to deter the rape of Kosovo; it was speeding it up. Publicly, NATO insisted that the blame for the hegira lay solely with Milosevic, not Western bombs. But privately, officials offered a line that made more sense alongside the awful images. Military planners lamented that bad weather, clever Serbian tactics, White House worries about collateral damage—and a reluctance to risk pilot's lives—kept them from hitting at Milosevic as hard as they wished.

The frustrated allies picked up the pace of the bombing, launched a precision cruise-missile attack that set key ministries in the heart of Belgrade aflame, and unleashed a massive pounding over the Easter weekend. And reluctantly, they began planning for a much broader campaign

against Milosevic, one that included the use of ground forces—a tactic President Clinton had assured Americans he would not sanction when NATO began bombing.

In Belgrade, young people proudly painted bull's-eye targets on their shirts and buildings. They rallied for Slobo in the same streets and squares where they had marched in protest in 1997 to bring him down. Serbs danced in jubilation on the wreckage of a U.S. F-117A fighter and gloated a few days later at the capture of three American soldiers, Staff Sergeant Andrew Ramirez, 24, Staff Sergeant Christopher Stone, 25, and Specialist Steven Gonzales, 21. (They were freed early in May after the Rev. Jesse Jackson, practicing his special brand of free-lance diplomacy, visited Belgrade and persuaded Milosevic to release them.)

Yet Milosevic's brutality also made him NATO's best ally. By displacing and deporting the Kosovars, he generated worldwide sympathy for the refugees and turned skeptical Americans into wary supporters of the operation. Pictures of thousands of refugees loaded into boxcars and stories of parents separated from their children helped NATO argue that the war was just and the enemy evil.

Meanwhile, a trio of deadly mishaps left NATO on the defensive. On April 12, two missiles intended to blow up a

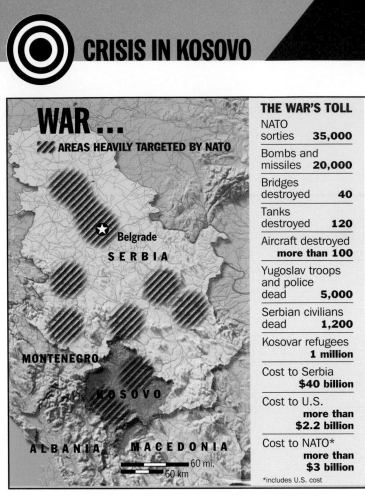

WAR...

▨ AREAS HEAVILY TARGETED BY NATO

SERBIA

★ Belgrade

MONTENEGRO

KOSOVO

ALBANIA   MACEDONIA

60 mi.
60 km

THE WAR'S TOLL

NATO sorties	**35,000**
Bombs and missiles	**20,000**
Bridges destroyed	**40**
Tanks destroyed	**120**
Aircraft destroyed	**more than 100**
Yugoslav troops and police dead	**5,000**
Serbian civilians dead	**1,200**
Kosovar refugees	**1 million**
Cost to Serbia	**$40 billion**
Cost to U.S.	**more than $2.2 billion**
Cost to NATO*	**more than $3 billion**

*includes U.S. cost

Serbian bridge across the Southern Morava River struck a train carrying civilians. At least 10 Serbs were killed, and 16 other passengers were badly injured. Two days later NATO at first denied its planes had savaged a convoy of fleeing Albanians inside Kosovo, then confessed the terrible error.

On May 7, another errant bombing provoked a major international crisis: an American B-2 bomber sent a trio of 2,000-lb. bombs into the Chinese embassy in Belgrade. Twenty civilians were wounded, and three journalists were killed. The embarrassing cause of the error: faulty U.S. intelligence information. The bombs were dropped to hit the nearby headquarters of Yugoslavia's weapons-buying and -development office.

The Chinese were furious. In Beijing the wife of U.S. Ambassador James Sasser was trapped in her residence by a mob of protesters; they smashed windows, pitched Molotov cocktails and threatened to break in, even as Sasser was trapped inside the embassy, half a mile away, by a similar mob. Though Clinton offered his "regrets and profound condolences," the bombing sent Chinese-American relations into a deep chill.

The allies stopped "ethnic cleansing," sent a moral message to the world, and smashed Serbia's war machine. But the bully was still boss in Belgrade

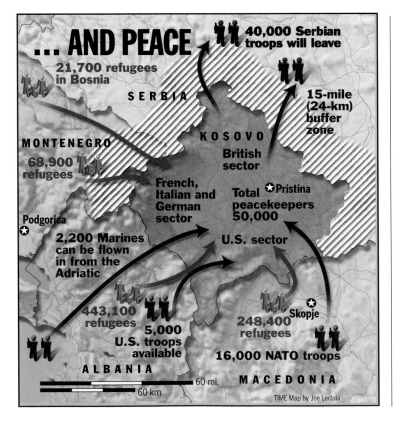

... AND PEACE

👥👥 **40,000 Serbian troops will leave**

21,700 refugees in Bosnia

SERBIA

15-mile (24-km) buffer zone

MONTENEGRO

68,900 refugees

KOSOVO

British sector

French, Italian and German sector

Total peacekeepers 50,000

⊛ Pristina

Podgorica ⊛

2,200 Marines can be flown in from the Adriatic

U.S. sector

443,100 refugees

5,000 U.S. troops available

248,400 refugees

⊛ Skopje

16,000 NATO troops

ALBANIA

MACEDONIA

60 mi.
60 km

TIME Map by Joe Lertola

Behind the scenes in Belgrade, quiet diplomacy was at work. On April 14, a few weeks after the bombing began, Russia sent special envoy Viktor Chernomyrdin on a shuttle mission to Milosevic; he spent many fruitless hours with the Serbian leader. But the peace talks were given a boost when the neutral President of Finland, Martti Ahtisaari, joined Chernomyrdin in urging a settlement. Finally, on June 2 the unpredictable Milosevic startled the world by abruptly ending the war and accepting all NATO demands—including a Serb withdrawal from Kosovo, NATO forces to ensure peace and eventual autonomy for the province—almost the exact terms he had rebuffed on March 23.

Why did Milosevic give in at last? It had been easy for him to ride out the first 30 days of air strikes, when bad weather and alliance timidity limited the damage to Serbia. But in the war's second month, NATO ratcheted up the pressure, launching 350 attack sorties every 24 hours. Bombs and missiles blitzed much of Serbia's heavy industry, energy sector and transport network. Citizen morale crumbled under water shortages and power outages. Protests broke out in the

PROTESTS: Left, U.S. Ambassador James Sasser after a Beijing protest. Right, 10,000 Kosovars denounce Serbia

smashed industrial cities of the south. The allies began holding serious talks about committing ground troops to the fray. And the Hague international war-crimes tribunal indicted Milosevic on May 24, placing his very life in jeopardy if he ever slipped from power.

It took 72 days of death and destruction to arrive back where the combatants had started: at the original precarious prescription for safeguarding the Kosovars. Except that now hundreds of thousands of them had been expelled from their wasted homeland, thousands had died, and untold others had been subjected to atrocious crimes. The West had acquired an unstable Kosovo protectorate that would require intensive military and political care for years to come, and an immense bill, in the billions of dollars, to reconstruct the ravaged economies of the Balkans.

NATO could be proud that it had hung together, stuck to its demands and lost not one soldier in combat—an unprecedented feat. The allies had stood up against barbaric "ethnic cleansing" and sent a moral lesson to the world. Serbia's war machine had been mutilated. American air power—including the controversial B-2 bomber, which performed beyond expectations—had vindicated itself.

Serbia was devastated by bombing, and the Serbian people had paid dearly in lost lives, lost jobs, lost hope. Yet the leader responsible was still secure in Belgrade. His divided opponents, aided by NATO, staged protests against his regime, to little effect. The Butcher of the Balkans—though a bully and a poor leader—is certainly a survivor. As long as Milosevic continues to infect his corner of Europe, the region may expect little peace. ∎

TO THE RESCUE: Kosovar children greet French helicopters arriving with aid at a camp near Kukes, northern Albania

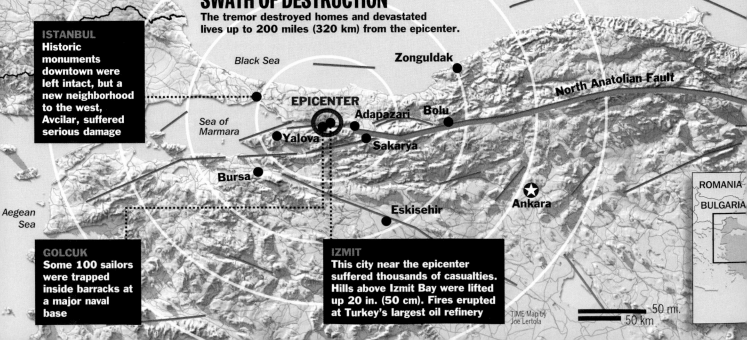

SWATH OF DESTRUCTION
The tremor destroyed homes and devastated
lives up to 200 miles (320 km) from the epicenter.

BULGARIA

Black Sea

Zonguldak

North Anatolian Fault

EPICENTER

Adapazari

Bolu

Sea of
Marmara

Yalova

Sakarya

Bursa

Eskisehir

Ankara ★

Aegean
Sea

ROMANIA
BULGARIA

ISTANBUL
Historic
monuments
downtown were
left intact, but a
new neighborhood
to the west,
Avcilar, suffered
serious damage

GOLCUK
Some 100 sailors
were trapped
inside barracks at
a major naval
base

IZMIT
This city near the epicenter
suffered thousands of casualties.
Hills above Izmit Bay were lifted
up 20 in. (50 cm). Fires erupted
at Turkey's largest oil refinery

TIME Map by
Joe Lertola

50 mi.
50 km

SIMON KWONG—REUTERS

Buried Alive

A giant earthquake in Turkey kills more than 16,000, while another monster topples towers in Taiwan

EVERY HOUR COUNTS WHEN PEOPLE ARE BURIED alive. At 3:02 a.m. on Aug. 17, the ground shook violently for 45 sec. under northwestern Turkey, entombing tens of thousands of sleeping families. As dawn broke, the fierce summer sun burned down on hundreds of square miles of earthquake-ravaged cities and towns. The densely populated industrial heartland lay in ruin, some 40,000 buildings smashed by nature's power into mounds of shattered concrete and sharp, mangled steel. Ghostly voices cried out from dark holes beneath the rubble, pleading for rescue.

In the race to save the living, men used bulldozers and jackhammers—even bare hands—to claw into the dangerously teetering piles. Disaster experts from abroad, volunteers from around the country, neighbors from the next street dug desperately to reach the faint sounds of life still echoing from the debris. Here a frail three-year-old girl was pulled out, barely moving but alive. There a woman was extricated, still breathing, after rescuers spent eight hours delicately prying away the fallen slabs that had buried her.

Two thousand dead. Four thousand dead. Ten thousand dead. Eight thousand injured ... 18,000 ... 34,000. As the tolls rose each day, the figures grew numbing, the magnitude of the disaster hard to grasp. Almost 100,000 Turks left homeless; $20 billion lost in property and production; a sense of despair overtaking the country. THE PEOPLE ARE HELPLESS, THE STATE IS HELPLESS, WE CAN'T EVEN FIND ANYWHERE TO PUT OUR DEAD, read the headline in the *Sabah* newspaper. The final toll of the 7.4-magnitude temblor: more than 16,000 dead.

Substandard apartment blocks boosted the death count. Newspapers blamed greedy contractors who used shoddy materials, slipshod methods and the help of corrupt officials to bypass building codes and ignore quakeproofing requirements. Block after block of flimsy flats, thrown up to accommodate rural migrants to the cities, collapsed, while solid buildings withstood the temblor with barely a crack.

Weeks later, on Sept. 21, an even bigger quake—magnitude 7.6—slammed into Taiwan. Centered near Puli, it left nearly 2,000 dead and at least 100,000 homeless and toppled some 6,000 buildings. Structures were peeled open like dollhouses, with walls stripped away and still-furnished rooms absurdly exposed to the air. The quake's aftershocks reverberated through today's tightly interwoven global economy. Taiwan produces more than 30% of the world's computer chip sets and motherboards, and the slowdown in supply threatened to roil the technology industry for months. ∎

- ▨ Major fault lines
- — Other fault lines
- ● Cities with major damage

FLATTENED: At top, an apartment building in Taiwan was collapsed onto its neighbors by the quake. Scientists believe the island nation is in line for more such events; it sits directly atop the juncture of two tectonic plates. Below, Emine Kacar of Izmit, Turkey, was trapped in her fallen building; she tried in vain to keep her children alive. It was Turkey's worst quake since 1939, when 30,000 people were killed

ERHAN SEVENLER—ANADOLU AGENCY—SIPA

RUSSIA

Sea

GEORGIA

Map area

Y

SYRIA

S

IRAQ

GESTURES OF DEFIANCE

A sect of quiet believers rattles the rulers of Beijing—and the crackdown is quick

THE EXERCISES HAD NAMES LIKE "GOLDEN MONKEY SPLITTING ITS Body" and "Two Dragons Entering the Sea." The practitioners were mostly pensioners, the unemployed and others not in the fast lane of today's get-rich China. They gathered every morning under the yellow-and-red banners of Falun Gong in parks across China to do the exercise routines and to meditate on the doctrines espoused by their leader, Li Hongzhi, 48. Li founded Falun Gong in 1992, fled China in 1998 and now lives in Manhattan. His teachings are a variant of *Qi Gong*, a blend of mind and body work (it also includes Tai Chi). The goal is to harness an inner energy called *qi*. It all seems harmless enough—yet in 1999 the cult provoked the toughest crackdown on human rights in China since the Tiananmen Square massacre 10 years before.

The members of Falun Gong first sent shudders through China's leaders on April 25, when some 10,000 of its members materialized on the sidewalk surrounding Beijing's Zhongnanhai government compound, demanding that the sect receive status as a permitted group.

The protest was serenely peaceful, but it was a protest nonetheless. What particularly frightened the leaders inside the compound was that so many people could assemble without the normally vigilant security services finding out. The police discovered that the demonstration was planned in large part by e-mail and that Falun Gong had a "virtual" organization linking its members. Beijing estimated that Falun Gong, founded in 1992, had 2 million adherents; the group claimed 100 million practitioners.

On July 22 the government banned the movement for practicing "evil thinking" and threatening social stability. Police detained thousands of the sect's followers, outlawed their traditional exercises and began destroying more than 2 million of their books and instruction tapes. Some 1,200 members were reportedly sent to a northern city for re-education. Li Hongzhi was branded a criminal and put on a "wanted" list. On Oct. 31, four leaders of the sect were arrested and formally charged with criminal acts.

But China's leaders were walking a tightrope: even as they cracked down on personal freedoms, they agreed for the first time to open their economy to outsiders, when they reached a landmark pact with U.S. Trade Representative Charlene Barshefsky in November. Under its terms, China would join the World Trade Organization and open its economy to foreign companies. The deal put a hopeful cap on a year that saw U.S. relations with China riding a seesaw. Charges of Chinese espionage in the spring (*see box*) were followed by a disappointing April visit to the U.S. by Chinese Premier Zhu Rongji. The trade agreement had been planned as the centerpiece of his trip, but it was derailed when President Clinton demanded changes. Only weeks later, an errant U.S. missile hit the Chinese embassy in Belgrade, and Beijing was outraged.

Americans hoped November's trade agreement would first open China's borders, then the minds of its leaders. For it seemed evident that China was a house divided, with its dictatorial rulers clinging to power and its people yearning to breathe free. ■

OPEN THE MARKET! China's Premier Zhu Rongji works on his trading signals at Chicago's Mercantile Exchange

SUE OGROCKI—REUTERS

THE CHINA SYNDROME
Did spies give U.S. nuclear secrets to Beijing?

The charges are chilling: for decades China has been running a major intelligence-collection effort targeting an array of U.S. military and commercial technologies. As a result, Beijing has acquired both by stealth and by legitimate means pieces of hardware and information that could accelerate modernization of its outmoded military. These findings were detailed in a 700-page report issued unanimously in May by a congressional committee chaired by California Republican Christopher Cox. Whether "understated," as Cox and many other Republicans claimed, or an exaggerated "worst case," as many intelligence experts and Democrats believed, the report sparked political fallout that imperiled U.S. relations with China.

The report's most compelling indictment was not of China but of the U.S. Lax security at national weapons labs, it charged, virtually invited Beijing to pick their pockets. For years officials ignored complaints that the labs were wide open, and no Administration bolstered their feeble protective measures. According to the report, Bill Clinton's predecessors had been embarrassingly oblivious to the spying under their noses, and once Clinton's team first got wind of the problem, they took an astonishingly long time to act. Critics said National Security Adviser Sandy Berger, who was briefed in 1996, deep-sixed the problem to get Clinton past the election.

Suspicion initially focused on Wen Ho Lee, a Taiwanese-born computer scientist who had worked for years on nuclear-warhead design programs at Los Alamos. Lee was suspected of divulging highly sensitive data on America's ultracompact W-88 warhead and other nuclear secrets. FBI and Justice Department agents wrangled over investigating Lee until 1999, when they finally got a look inside his hard drive. They were appalled to discover he had downloaded the "legacy codes," containing all the most important data the U.S. had amassed from years of nuclear testing, onto his unclassified computer. Department of Energy Secretary Bill Richardson fired Lee in March, but he was not arrested until December. In late fall the FBI began to focus its attention on outside companies that work with Los Alamos in weapons development, suggesting they feared espionage by a number of sources.

Both countries have too much to lose to let their budding economic and cultural relationship rupture. For its part, China strenuously denied all the charges, which could disrupt the delicate balancing act that keeps Sino-American relations from spinning out of control—and into a new cold war.

EXIT THE

Boris Yeltsin pulls a vanishing act on New Year's Eve, handing over Russia's reins to an untested heir

ON THE EVE OF A 1998 VISIT TO ROME, BORIS YELTSIN chided a group of Italian journalists graced with a Kremlin audience. "It's a pity your Prime Ministers change so often," he said. "It makes things complicated ..." Indeed. Things certainly became complicated in Russia in 1999. On Aug. 9, Yeltsin (the advocate of stability) fired Sergei Stepashin—his fourth Prime Minister in 17 months—after he had been in office only 82 days. (Keeping score? Stepashin's predecessor, Yevgeni Primakov, was canned in May.) To replace him, Yeltsin named Vladimir Putin—a virtual unknown to most Russians—deeming Putin his political heir in the upcoming March 2000 presidential election. Months later, the ailing autocrat of the Kremlin topped that surprise: he stunned the world on New Year's Eve by resigning his office and handing power over to the enigmatic Putin.

A slight, contained man, Putin, 47, is a veteran of Soviet intelligence. Although he spent 15 years in East Germany as a KGB operative, then served as a top aide to reforming mayor Anatoly Sobchak in St. Petersburg, little was known of him. When a TV interviewer asked Putin for "a few words" about his family in August, he gave her a few: "Wife, two children. Two girls, 13 and 14 years old." His curtness masked his real nature, colleagues said; they claimed he was a tough guy, but an enlightened, modern one.

The enlightened man inherited a mess. In mid-June, Shamil Basayev, a brilliant strategist who helped command Chechen forces during the victorious 1994-96 war with Russia, led 2,000 fighters from Chechnya into neighboring Dagestan, a tiny Muslim republic of 2.1 million people and more than 30 ethnic groups, in an attempt to establish a new Muslim imamate. Russian troops drove them out, but a new incursion followed in late July. Meanwhile, terrorist Muslims from the Caucasus were accused of having triggered a series of deadly late-summer bombings in Moscow; a war against them would serve both

ILLUSTRATION FOR TIME BY ISMAEL ROLDAN

PUPPET MASTER

NEW BOSS: Putin visits Chechnya

Yeltsin and Putin. In Russia, hatred of the Chechens spans political chasms between hard-line nationalists and pro-Western liberals: now all could unite behind their indivisible motherland. By October, the Kremlin had succeeded in plunging the entire region back into full-scale war.

At year's end, Russian troops had marched through Chechnya's sparsely settled northern plains and were meeting strong resistance in Grozny, the capital. As the macho Putin's popularity in opinion polls soared, it seemed the war against Chechen terrorism was his platform for the upcoming elections. But he wouldn't need one: on Dec. 19, the political bloc the Kremlin feared most, former Prime Minister Primakov's Fatherland–All Russia Party, was beaten into a disappointing third place in parliamentary elections. The way was clear for Yeltsin to resign.

The President's farewell speech left the impression of a despondent, ailing leader who had been persuaded, gently but firmly, that it was time to go. The resignation was planned with one end in mind—Putin's elevation would protect Yeltsin, his family and their close associates, who were being investigated by a corps of Swiss prosecutors that had been probing allegations of Kremlin financial malfeasance involving a Swiss construction firm. Before leaving the stage, the puppet master had to ensure that a successor wouldn't be pursuing him or his family. Indeed, Putin's actions in his first hours as President included a guarantee of immunity from prosecution for the man who first pulled his strings. ■

A BITTER REPLAY: Only three short years after Chechnya repelled a demoralized, poorly equipped and incompetently led Russian army to achieve de facto independence, the breakaway province was again a battleground. This time the Russians called the invasion an "antiterrorist operation."

By late December, Russian troops controlled Chechnya's second city, Gudermes, and were meeting serious resistance in the capital, Grozny. Chechnya's President, Aslan Maskhadov, had little power over strong local warlords. Above, a Russian chopper crashes near the Chechen border

Promoting the General's Welfare

Should Uncle Sam smile when military bosses overthrow democratic rule?

EXUBERANCE: Cheering Pakistanis hail the downfall of Nawaz Sharif's government

MILITARY COUPS USED TO BE MESSY AFFAIRS, RIFE WITH panic, barricades and bloodshed. Yet most Pakistanis barely shrugged at the overthrow of their democratically elected government in October. In the span of 48 hours, army chief General Pervez Musharraf detained Prime Minister Nawaz Sharif, sacked the Cabinet, suspended Parliament and the constitution, and imposed virtual martial law. Yet shops remained open. Telephone service was restored. Children went to school. In Sharif's hometown of Lahore, rejoicing citizens danced in the streets and distributed candies to celebrate the coup. "We don't want democracy," said Mohammed Tariq, 22, a taxi driver in the capital, Islamabad. "We just want law and order and stable prices."

Most Pakistanis agreed. Militant Islamists tied to Afghanistan's Taliban government hailed the downfall of Sharif, who before his fall had clamped down on fundamentalist groups inside Pakistan following a spasm of sectarian violence that left 40 dead. Former Prime Minister Benazir Bhutto, twice sacked for alleged corruption, praised the junta for removing Sharif.

Even in Western capitals, including Washington, the usual jitters were tempered by widespread relief that Sharif was gone. The Asian subcontinent has been a source of heightened anxiety for the U.S. since the spring of 1998, when India tested nuclear devices and Pakistan responded with its own nuclear tests. The two countries' dispute over the territory of Kashmir had brought them to the brink of all-out war in the spring and summer of '99. The Clinton Administration prodded Sharif to scale back his army's adventurism in Kashmir and exacted his cooperation in cracking down on terrorist training cells in Afghanistan. But Washington had come to believe that Sharif was digging his own grave.

Still, the coup did not solve the problems that make the region one of the most dangerous places on earth. While Musharraf is a liberal Muslim and most of the army's top brass are moderate, U.S. analysts say fundamentalists have made inroads in the lower ranks of the military. A rise in fundamentalism under the new regime could set off another wave of sectarian killings and unnerve India. Preoccupied with national elections, Indians responded warily to the coup and returned Prime Minister Atal Behari Vajpayee's Hindu-nationalist Bharatiya Janata Party party to power.

Pakistanis are used to army rule. The military has run the country for 25 of the 52 years since the birth of the nation in the 1947 partition from India. An early period of military rule led to civil war, armed confrontation with India, and the independence of Bangladesh in 1971. There was little longing for the military's return to power, but action became inevitable after Sharif returned from a July meeting with President Clinton in Washington and ordered the military to retreat from the Indian side of Kashmir, infuriating army commanders.

General Musharraf does not fit the profile of a strongman: he is known as a principled consensus builder

General Musharraf does not fit the profile of a strongman. He is known as a quiet, principled consensus builder who has modest political ambitions. His son lives in the U.S., and in his free time, Musharraf is said to read the speeches of Abraham Lincoln. The world will be watching to see if he can foster a government of the people, by the people and for the people—under martial law. ■

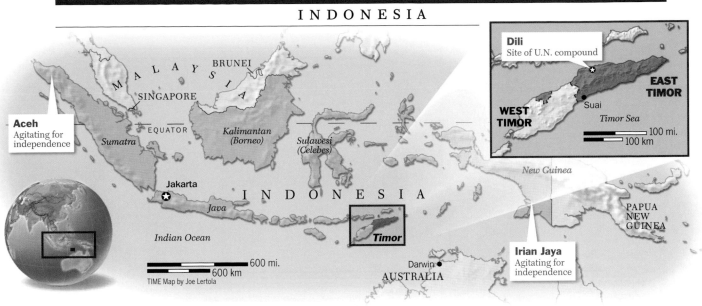

Aceh
Agitating for
independence

Dili
Site of U.N. compound

WEST
TIMOR

EAST
TIMOR

Suai

Timor Sea

100 mi.
100 km

New Guinea

PAPUA
NEW
GUINEA

Timor

Irian Jaya
Agitating for
independence

Darwin ●
AUSTRALIA

600 mi.
600 km
TIME Map by Joe Lertola

Freedom's Price

East Timor declares its independence in signatures of blood, as Indonesia weathers a risky passage to democracy

FOR SEVERAL HORRIFYING WEEKS IN THE SUMMER OF 1999, Indonesia's breakaway province of East Timor became a killing field. Within hours of the Sept. 4 announcement that nearly 80% of the electorate had voted for independence in an Aug. 30 referendum, the capital city of Dili and other towns echoed with gunfire as militiamen took over the streets, unchecked by the military. Civilians poured into churches, convents and U.N. compounds seeking safety. Priests and nuns were among those singled out for execution as shops, churches, radio stations and clinics were torched. Some 200,000 people—as much as a quarter of the population—fled the territory. Finally, after a four-week rampage, Indonesian President B.J. Habibie submitted to boiling international pressure and agreed to allow U.N. peacekeepers into East Timor.

Hints of the madness to come had been apparent since January. When Habibie unexpectedly offered locals a referendum on independence in January, militia groups who wanted continued ties with Jakarta began to organize and acquire guns. Even before the vote, supporters of independence were intimidated and dozens killed. Although the militias were clearly buttressed by elements of the Indonesian armed forces, the international community in May entrusted security during the referendum period to Indonesia—a fatal misjudgment.

Violence is not new to East Timor. Colonized by the Portuguese in the 16th century for its sandalwood, and predominantly Catholic, it was invaded by Indonesian troops in December 1975 with the tacit consent of the U.S. Some 200,000 East Timorese died in the occupation; the annexation of the territory was never recognized by the U.N.

The chaos brought Habibie down; he withdrew from Indonesia's first-ever democratic elections in October. Voters chose a blind Muslim cleric, Abdurrahman Wahid, as President—and the canny scholar brought a bitterly divided nation together when he engineered the selection of his chief rival, Megawati Sukarnoputri, as his Vice President. Megawati, daughter of deposed strongman Suharto, commanded the allegiance of her father's many followers.

In the 18 months since Suharto was forced to resign and named Habibie to succeed him, Indonesia had lurched repeatedly from giddy euphoria to violent despair and back. The good news: despite the ethnic violence and looting in major cities and the carnage in East Timor, this sprawling archipelago of 210 million people never disintegrated into civil war. Instead, Indonesia completed its transition from a military-backed dictatorship to the world's third largest democracy. But the price was steep. ■

JOHN STANMEYER—SABA FOR TIME (2)

ANARCHY RULES: A rock-wielding East Timorese is killed by Jakarta-backed militiamen

Images

SPIRAL SPLENDOR Marking the return of its capital to Berlin 10 years after the fall of the Wall, a unified Germany opened its renovated Reichstag, seat of the parliament. The $330 million make-over, designed by Briton Sir Norman Foster, sports a glass dome with a spiral ramp that allows people to climb to its top (and look down on their legislators). Foster kept much of the history of the 19th century edifice, including damage to its walls from the 1933 fire, World War II bombing raids and graffiti left by Russian soldiers who captured it in 1945.

A Fresh Start in Israel

The year in the Mideast may be said to have begun not on Jan. 1 but on May 17. That was the day Ehud Barak, once an ill-adapted politician disparaged in his own Labor Party, trounced Likud incumbent Benjamin Netanyahu, who had been mythologized as invincible. Barak took 56% of the vote, a huge majority in a country where the two main parties usually break even. An unlikely campaigner for peace, Barak is Israel's most highly decorated soldier, a planner of the famous 1976 hostage rescue at Uganda's Entebbe airport.

Barak's mandate gave him the authority to reverse Netanyahu's policies of division and obstruction and energetically pursue peace with Israel's Arab neighbors. And he did, visiting Washington in July to cement a relationship with Bill Clinton, then meeting with Yasser Arafat and Clinton in Oslo in November in hopes of getting the peace process back on track. In October Barak stunned hard-core Israelis by beginning to dismantle some settlements in the occupied territories. There was even talk of a deal with his nation's most bitterly intransigent enemy in the region, Syria's Hafez Assad.

ON TRACK: Arafat and Barak grip and grin in Oslo

JERRY LAMPEN—REUTERS

NEW BOSS: Jordan's Abdullah

BARRY IVERSON FOR TIME

Jordan's New Ruler

For 34 years King Hussein's brother Hassan had been Jordan's King-in-waiting. But in a span of a few hours the week before his death, Hussein sent Hassan an angry dismissal, accusing him of power grabbing. The dying King then installed his untested eldest son Abdullah, 37, as heir to the Hashemite throne. Though clearly galled by the decision, Hassan, 51, quickly affirmed his loyalty to Abdullah, who was crowned in June.

Now, Ballistic Extortion

When you can't beat 'em, bribe 'em: so goes policy in North Korea. On the brink of collapse and with its people racked by starvation, the nation's most successful business involved pulling cash and aid out of South Korea, the U.S. and Japan in exchange for abandoning an arms buildup. This year's wrinkle in high-priced extortion: the threatened test launch of a ballistic missile that could finger the very outer edges of America. This time Uncle Sam called "Dear Leader" Kim Jong Il's bluff, vowing

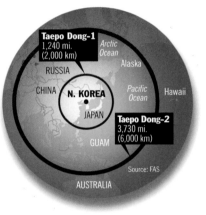

Taepo Dong-1
1,240 mi.
(2,000 km)

Arctic Ocean

Alaska

RUSSIA

CHINA   N. KOREA

Pacific Ocean

Hawaii

JAPAN

Taepo Dong-2
3,730 mi.
(6,000 km)

GUAM

Source: FAS

AUSTRALIA

WOLFGANG KUMM—CORBIS AFP

to cut off financial and humanitarian aid if the missile was tested. Pyongyang made rude noises but backed down. Yet the fact remains that America's most vexing internal problem—nuts with guns—has a more frightening corollary in Asia: a maniac with a missile.

NO MERCY: A member of a Hutu death squad

ABDELHAK SENNS—AFP

TIM GRAHAM—CORBIS SYGMA

CHEERIO! Edward and Sophie

Northern Ireland's Day

The peace accord reached on Good Friday, 1998, stalled for months in Northern Ireland, but the year ended in decisive change after former U.S. Senator George Mitchell brokered a breakthrough. In late November, pro-British Protestants of the Ulster Unionist Party voted to allow the Sinn Fein party into the region's nascent government without first disarming its I.R.A. military wing. On Dec. 2, authority over Northern Ireland officially passed from London to Belfast's new Protestant-Catholic government. The I.R.A. agreed to disarm by May 2000.

Horror in Uganda

The tourists had come in hopes of seeing a few of the world's 600 remaining mountain gorillas at play. But just after dawn on March 1, 100 Rwandan Hutu, brandishing guns and machetes, attacked the travelers, seizing 14 people. Only six returned alive. The rest, including two vacationers from Oregon, were bludgeoned and hacked to death. The Hutu oppose U.S. and British support of Uganda's regime.

People

Welcome to "The Firm"

Poor Prince Edward: by the time Queen Elizabeth's youngest son took a bride in June, all the allusions to fairy-tale princesses and royal happily-ever-afters had been used and then discredited by her other children. Conveniently, the new couple, Edward Windsor and Sophie Rhys-Jones, appear to be down-to-earth. With her own public relations company, Sophie, 34, is more mature than either the naive Diana or the coltish Fergie when they married into the family "firm." And Edward, 35, has launched a career as a TV producer.

On June 19, Edward and his groomsmen brothers, Princes Charles and Andrew, were greeted by 8,000 cheering locals outside and 550 invited guests inside St. George's Chapel at Windsor Castle. Despite its vaulted grandeur, the chapel was chosen for its relative intimacy; the couple wanted a low-key affair.

Onlookers applauded when Sophie arrived with her father, a former tire salesman. Considerably less crinolined than the dresses of Diana and Sarah, Sophie's fitted silk-organza-and-crepe gown nevertheless boasted 325,000 cut-glass and pearl beads and a formidable train. Her veil was affixed with a diamond tiara borrowed from the Queen.

In pointed, if understated, opposition to Diana Spencer and Sarah Ferguson, Sophie promised that she would "obey" her husband.

Space Imaging—Reuters

With telecommunications companies leading the year's merger stampede, the business world may for once have lived up to its boilerplate boasts of "big pictures" and "sweeping visions." Yet one company proved too big for its britches: a federal judge found that Microsoft was a monopoly that had abused its power.

PRIVATE EYE IN THE SKY: The nation's capital, as seen from a satellite owned by Space Imaging, Inc. In 1999 it became the first company to harness spy-satellite technology for commercial use.

Business

What's next for monopolist Gates? "Baby Bills"? Separation anxiety? Red tape?

ON FRIDAY, NOVEMBER 5, at 4:30 p.m., an attorney from the antitrust division of the Justice Department with a hot-off-the-presses copy of the Microsoft decision in his hands called his boss from a Washington courthouse. "What does it say?" asked an eager Joel Klein. "I'm on page 16," said the lawyer, "and it says they're a monopolist." "Great!" Klein rejoiced. "Keep reading!"

sented Gates as a law-flouting monopolist who threatened, berated and retaliated against his rivals.

As the sweep of Judge Jackson's ruling became clear, the anti-Microsoft camp was gleeful. James Barksdale, the folksy former Netscape CEO who testified at the trial that Microsoft tried to suffocate his company, hailed the findings as "an 11 on a 10-point scale." Klein, flanked by Attorney General Janet Reno at a celebratory press conference, declared that it "shows once again that in America, no person and no company is above the law."

Microsoft for its part deployed legions of spinners to argue that Jackson had it all wrong. The company had broken no laws and done no harm to consumers. The judge failed to appreciate the dynamic nature of the software business, which makes any dominant position inherently short lived. The only lapse in Microsoft's genetic self-assurance was a video press release the company rushed on the air after the ruling. "We hope we can find a way," Gates declared, "to resolve this and put it behind us." For a moment he seemed to be waving the white flag of settlement. And one could

REBOOTING MICROSOFT

And so, in 1999's last months, Microsoft Corp. joined Standard Oil and AT&T on the list of the 20th century's great monopolies. After the Justice Department squared off against Bill Gates & Co. in 1998, it was no secret that things were going badly for Bill. But even so, the findings of fact that Judge Thomas Penfield Jackson handed down were stunning in their breadth and their certainty: a blunt 412-paragraph *j'accuse* that nailed Microsoft not only on the two most critical issues—that it had monopoly control over PC operating systems and that it wielded that power in ways that harmed American consumers—but on virtually every count brought against it.

Microsoft could not have come out much worse. The ruling carefully laid out the factual basis for the major antitrust violations that seemed certain to follow. And it painted an exceedingly dark portrait of one of America's most admired companies. The Microsoft of Judge Jackson's narrative is a deep-pocketed bully that used "its prodigious market power and immense profits to harm" companies that presumed to compete with it. Jackson pre-

come: two weeks after issuing his findings of fact, Judge Jackson appointed a respected federal appeals judge, Richard Posner, as a mediator to seek an agreement between Justice and Microsoft.

Unless he brokered a settlement, there could be a lot more bad news coming Gates' way. Jackson still had to issue conclusions of law—expected early in 2000—in which he would use these facts to decide if Microsoft employed its monopoly power to violate the antitrust laws. If he says yea—a near certainty considering his findings—he could impose a remedy as far-reaching as the total dismemberment of the Gates empire. And more potential bad news: these findings of fact could be used by a host of competitors to bring their own civil antitrust actions against Microsoft. Three California lawyers announced in late November they'd bring a class-action suit against Microsoft on behalf of consumers; it could be the first of a flood of such suits. The reverberations of the case will be felt for some time throughout the high-tech world—and by the millions of Americans who have a stake in the battle because they own Microsoft stock.

MICROSOFT: THE REMEDIES

What will Justice do to break up the Microsoft monopoly if no settlement is reached? Here are four scenarios:

MICROSOFT SANS WINDOWS: Force Microsoft to spill its most treasured possession, the source code for Windows. This might be auctioned to other companies, which could then go out and sell their own versions. Or the code could simply be declared public property and given away.
Who wins? Open-source advocates, who say all operating-system source codes should be freely available (as Linux's is). The public might benefit if competition led to innovation. It could be harmed if software became even more confusing than it already is.

UNLEASH THE BABY BILLS: Cut the company vertically, into two or three little Microsofts. Each would continue to make and sell the full range of Microsoft software. Indistinguishable clones would probably end up confusing the marketplace. And given Microsoft's history of corporate acquisitiveness, how long would it take for one of the Baby Bills to swallow up the others?
Who wins? Whichever company gets Bill. Also Linux, Apple OS and any other competing operating system—if consumers sour on Windows PCs.

CARVE IT INTO LITTLE PIECES: Cut the company along neater lines so that one Baby Bill markets Windows, the next sells office software, etc. However, a recent reorganization of Microsoft's internal divisions will make this option more difficult than it once would have been.
Who wins? Whichever company gets Windows, whose monopoly of the operating-systems market is what Microsoft has been leveraging all along.

TIE IT UP IN RED TAPE: Make Microsoft sign agreements to separate its operating system (Windows) from its Web browser (Explorer), or to sell Windows to all computer makers at the same price regardless of their relationship with Microsoft.
Who wins? Microsoft. Critics point out that this is precisely what the Justice Department tried to do in its 1994 consent decree with Microsoft, and look how much good that did.

TRUST BUSTERS: Janet Reno, lead lawyer David Boies and Joel Klein (rear) meet the press after their victory

The finding that Microsoft was a monopoly was a legal no-brainer, once the court accepted the government's narrow definition of the relevant market: PC operating-systems software. If Microsoft—which controlled more than 90% of that market—wasn't a monopoly, then nobody was. Microsoft tried to argue that its Windows operating system was under constant threat and could be made obsolete at any moment. But the competitors it listed hardly seemed like giant-killers. Upstart Linux, the open-source operating system that Microsoft spoke of so fearfully, ran less than 3% of all PCs in 1999. Even if you included Apple, which was undeniably on an upswing, Microsoft still had more than 80% of the small-computer market.

The ruling went on to detail the ways in which Microsoft used its monopoly power to bludgeon the competition. If you liked the trial, you'd love the judge's greatest-hits collection of Microsoft skulduggery: binding its Internet Explorer browser into Windows just to beat out Netscape; bullying Intel into staying out of the software market; polluting Sun Microsystems' Java programming language to diminish the competitive threat it posed to Windows; threatening IBM. And Compaq. And Apple.

Microsoft likes to say its hypercompetitive business practices only hurt rivals, not consumers. But Jackson found that Microsoft was so quick to crush any perceived threats that countless technology products that should have been developed died stillborn. "The ultimate result," he wrote, "is that some innovations that would truly benefit consumers never occur for the sole reason that they do not coincide with Microsoft's self-interest." Even more devastating, Jackson found that in its rush to make life tough for its competitors, Microsoft was actually willing to diminish the quality of its own products. Bundling a Web browser into Windows 98 did not benefit consumers, as Microsoft claimed. Rather, Jackson found, it slowed down the operating system, increased the likelihood of a crash and made it easier for "malicious viruses" to find their way from the Internet onto our computers. Ouch.

The decision was a blueprint for finding that Microsoft did indeed willfully and repeatedly violate the Sherman Antitrust Act. If Microsoft was found to have violated the law, then what? Klein and his troops scrupulously avoided talking about a remedy (though they had experts on retainer for months sorting through the options). The gamut of possible outcomes runs from a mild go-forth-and-sin-no-more to the truly Draconian stuff: forcing Microsoft to share its Windows source code with its competitors or carving up the company into the so-called Baby Bills (*see box*).

The schedule called for a verdict by Feb. 1, 2000—unless a settlement was reached before. If not, an appeal was expected. The D.C. Circuit Court of Appeals, which would review Jackson's decision and remedy orders, is the same one that slapped the judge down in 1998 when he ordered Microsoft to offer Windows 95 without the Internet Explorer browser. The Supreme Court is harder to predict, although its pro-business tilt suggested the government might get a skeptical hearing. But neither was likely to overturn Jackson's findings of fact.

Are lawsuits like this good for the country? Microsoft's defenders said no. Bill Gates drops out of college to found a little start-up that, by his 44th birthday, has grown into the most valuable company in the world. His success ensures that the U.S. is in the forefront of a global technological revolution, and he produces a product used by millions. His reward for living the American Dream? Some smart Washington lawyers try to brand him a lawbreaker. By bringing lawsuits like this one, Microsoft's adherents argued, the government was meddling dangerously with private industry and thus the health of the entire U.S. economy.

Supporters of antitrust law argued that decisions like Judge Jackson's actually strengthen the free market. The new economy—and America's unprecedented run of growth and prosperity—was fueled to a significant degree by small start-ups founded by entrepreneurs with big dreams. These are precisely the sort of companies that could be crushed most easily by a brutal monop-

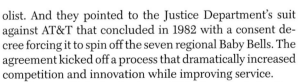

If Microsoft—which controlled 90% of its market—wasn't a monopoly, then nobody was

olist. And they pointed to the Justice Department's suit against AT&T that concluded in 1982 with a consent decree forcing it to spin off the seven regional Baby Bells. The agreement kicked off a process that dramatically increased competition and innovation while improving service.

How would the battle play out? The lawyers, Judge Posner and/or the appeals courts would have a say. But ultimately, the most important actor in this drama would be Bill Gates. When he was a kid, he and his family loved to play games, both intellectual and athletic. All of them were competitive, but Bill most of all. "The play was serious," his father recalled. "Winning mattered." Judge Jackson may have ruled against Gates—but don't rule him out quite yet. ■

MEANWHILE, THE BIG GET BIGGER

The Justice Department declared it sued Microsoft because it sought to encourage competition. Yet several giant deals in 1999 sped up consolidation in the telecommunications and media industries—but were not challenged by the department. Among them:

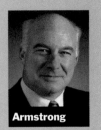

Armstrong

AT&T/MEDIAONE: In May, AT&T announced a $60 billion acquisition of cable company MediaOne and a $5 billion partnership with Microsoft, jump-starting AT&T chairman C. Michael Armstrong's ambitious plan to remake the famously ponderous long-distance telephone company into a new-economy supernova. The goal: to recast a rejuvenated Ma Bell as a benevolent Ma Everything, offering local and long-distance telephone service, high-speed Internet access and new television options like video on demand, all bundled into one coaxial cable.

Sumner Redstone, Mel Karmazin

VIACOM/CBS: Why did Sumner Redstone's Viacom Corp. merge with Mel Karmazin's CBS television network? "He seduced me," explained a smitten Redstone. (And you thought Rupert Murdoch and his new young wife were the year's hottest business couple.) The September affair paired the largely fuddy-duddy CBS assets—broadcast television, outdoor and radio advertising—with Viacom's hipper, younger, cable and movie-studio properties—MTV, VH1, Nickelodeon and Paramount Pictures. The $70 billion deal was billed as a merger of equals, although Viacom was clearly the acquiring party. The deal resolved another concern: Redstone, 76, though in fine fettle, had no clear successor. Karmazin, 56, and a darling of Wall Street, filled the bill.

MCI WORLDCOM/SPRINT: As telecommunications companies raced to get bigger, no one was running faster than the acquisitive Bernie Ebbers. The onetime boss of WorldCom, who had already devoured MCI and more than 60 other firms, announced in November that he would buy longtime rival Sprint, headed by William T. Esrey, for a cool $129 billion.

William Esrey, Bernie Ebbers

IN THE MARKETS, NOTHING BUT NET

They're up, they're down—roller-coaster Net stocks drive the markets as initial public offerings create instant gazillionaires

STEWART: Next, folding trade chits into origami bulls?

SOARING STOCKS OF INTERNET COMPANIES DEFIED convention and gravity in 1997 and '98. In 1999 things got more interesting: the one-way elevator heading up became a roller-coaster ride, as the Net stocks rose early in the year only to take a couple of vertiginous swoops in the summer, leaving investors feeling queasy and critics feeling vindicated. Yet after a slump that lasted several months, many of the Net stocks roared back in the fall.

Why the comeback? Never mind that to these outfits, profit is mostly a concept. They had cool products, hip clients, catchy names, irreverent ads, promise—lots of promise—and more. They had panache. They were cocktail chatter, and their stockholders were giddy. The money-losing online bookseller Amazon.com long ago had blown past venerable Sears in terms of market value. At the time, investors gasped and marveled. They kept buying, but at least they'd paused for thought. By April 1999, though, Amazon's worth was approaching that of Sears and Wal-Mart combined, and few were querying its balance sheet.

They paid attention in a hurry when the bottom fell out in early summer. Amazon's April apex, it turned out, was a high point in the market for Internet stocks. On average, they had declined 32% by mid-June, and many, including Amazon, had halved. Critics of the Net stocks cheered, claiming the bubble had finally burst. They were already classifying the Net mania with other historic flameouts, such as biotechnology (1980s), computer leasing (1970s) and, yes, those infamous tulips in Holland (1600s).

But leapin' Lazarus: reports of the death of the Net stocks were greatly exaggerated. The Web wonders were just taking a breather before a buoyant revival in the fall. The message: they were going to behave differently, as this industry, like so many before it, continued to evolve and develop. The future will include the creation of tons of stock as new initial public offerings (IPOs) flood the market in search of easy money (yours). And it will include the inevitable shakeout as investors sort the jewels from the junk. The only question is, How fast will all this happen?

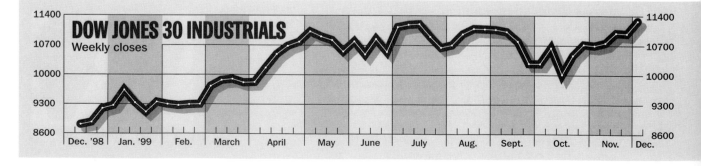

DOW JONES 30 INDUSTRIALS
Weekly closes

PETER MORGAN—REUTERS

If anything symbolized the public's lust for new stocks, it was the IPO, the moment when fledgling companies first offer their shares for sale on the market. Through November, 501 companies had launched IPOs in 1999, and their shares had soared an average of 62% on the first day of trading, more than three times the first-day gain in any other year in the roaring 1990s. A dozen of the stocks quadrupled, and 22 others tripled in a single day from the prices at which they were initially offered. Whoopee!

The IPO madness climaxed on Oct. 19, when an unlikely pair of stocks—those of homemaking doyen Martha Stewart and the highly popular World Wrestling Federation—made their market debuts. Stewart's shares, initially offered at $18, ended the day at $35^{9}/$_{16}$, and Martha hit the silk sheets that night worth $1.06 billion. WWF shares, initially offered at $17, closed at a less gaudy $25.

The market's fascination with Net and software stocks wasn't confined to IPOs. As buyers continued to pour money into a broad range of computer, technology and information companies, the index of the tech-heavy NASDAQ exchange surged to new records, busting through the symbolic 3000 barrier on Nov. 4.

Meanwhile, back in Wall Street's Dow Jones corral, the bulls were still riding high in 1999, if not quite as wide and handsome as in '97 and '98. With Uncle Sam running a surplus and unemployment levels at new lows, the index in early December hovered around 11,000, a 16% rise over its 1998 finish. In a nod to the age of global e-trading, the Big Board was even looking at staying open late into the evening. Who says you can't teach an old bull new tricks? ■

AOL
Apr. 16...69^{7}/$_{8}$
Aug. 6....42^{3}/$_{8}$
Dec. 1....76^{1}/$_{8}$

E*Trade
Apr. 16...46^{9}/$_{32}$
Aug. 6....25^{3}/$_{4}$
Dec. 1....30^{5}/$_{8}$

Priceline
Apr. 16... 81^{3}/$_{8}$
Aug. 6..... 74^{3}/$_{8}$
Dec. 1.....60^{5}/$_{8}$

iVillage
Apr. 16...97
Aug. 6....31
Dec. 1.....29

DoubleClick
Apr. 16..138^{1}/$_{16}$
Aug. 6......74
Dec. 1...170^{7}/$_{16}$

Amazon
Apr. 16...95
Aug. 6....44^{25}/$_{32}$
Dec. 1.....85

Sun MicroSystems
Apr. 16...54^{15}/$_{16}$
Aug. 6.....70^{1}/$_{2}$
Dec. 1...130^{3}/$_{16}$

Cisco
Apr. 16...52^{27}/$_{32}$
Aug. 6.....62^{1}/$_{4}$
Dec. 1....91^{7}/$_{16}$

eBay
Apr. 16...176
Aug. 6.....83^{1}/$_{4}$
Dec. 1....160

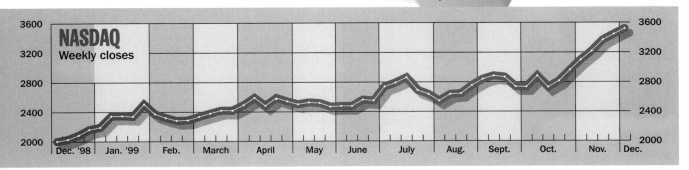

NASDAQ
Weekly closes

| Dec. '98 | Jan. '99 | Feb. | March | April | May | June | July | Aug. | Sept. | Oct. | Nov. | Dec. |

Smashing Through the Glass Ceiling

Women are named to lead Avon and Hewlett-Packard, but it's lonely at the top for lady execs

PAY NO ATTENTION TO THE NOISE, CARLETON ("Carly") Fiorina was saying in July, as she was crashing through the highest of glass ceilings to become the CEO of computer maker Hewlett-Packard. Although her appointment was not so ballyhooed as Sandra Day O'Connor's becoming the first woman Supreme Court Justice or Geraldine Ferraro's running for Vice President—or, for that matter, the U.S. team's winning the women's soccer World Cup—it was arguably more important than any of those milestones. If women have made great strides in gaining parity in politics and sports, it is in the workplace that sexism is most keenly felt. Women still earn 75% of men's salaries and occupy only 11.2% of the executive jobs in FORTUNE 500 companies. The top spot at HP, a geek kingdom since its birth in the slide-rule era, is the highest position ever held by a woman in a Dow 30 company.

"No woman has achieved leadership at this level of American business," said Sheila Wellington, president of Catalyst, a New York City organization that tracks women in the work force. "It's going to give young women, girls, a powerful message." It was even something of a Cinderella story: Fiorina had once worked as a secretary at HP.

"My gender is interesting, but it is not the story here," insisted Fiorina, 44. She preferred instead to put the focus on her considerable achievements as an executive with AT&T and its Lucent Technologies spin-off, where she enjoyed a remarkable run as president of the $20 billion Global Services division. She was partly responsible for re-engineering Lucent, once Ma Bell's lowly phonemaker, into a technology highflyer. Lucent is now a leading global sup-

HP's Carly Fiorina

plier of cell-phone networking gear and the digital-switching systems that are critical components of voice and data networks—you know, the Internet. She even helped design the red-swirl logo that marks Lucent as a leading-edge company.

At HP, Fiorina faces a slew of similar challenges as a company renowned for its engineering proficiency takes on fleet competitors like Dell and Sun Microsystems, which have decidedly jazzier images. "The old joke about HP is they'd market sushi as cold, dead fish," said Merrill Lynch analyst Steve Milonovich. "Right now they just don't have much of an Internet aura."

The sound of breaking glass was heard again in November, when Andrea Jung, 41, was named chief executive officer of Avon Products, moving up from president and chief operating officer. That Avon chose Jung had its own delicious twist: less than 18 months before, the cosmetics giant had passed her over and named Duracell CEO Charles Perrin president, even though he had no experience in direct selling or makeup. The Chinese-American Jung, a Princeton graduate, told the New York *Times:* "I'm proud of my heritage and certainly my gender."

Jung and Fiorina joined Marion Sandler at Golden West Financial and the embattled Jill Barad at slumping Mattel as capitalism's lonely Gang of Four, the only women chief executives of FORTUNE 500 companies. A 1999 Catalyst survey of female executives found that women made up 5.1% of so-called clout positions—chief executive down to chief vice president. Women also accounted for 11.9% of corporate officers, an improvement from 8.7% in 1995. And women were starting to catch up in pay as well: Catalyst said that in 1999 women accounted for 3.3% of top earners, the five best-paid executives at a company, up from 1.2% in 1995. The glass ceiling was still firmly in place—but easier to see, thanks to its new cracks. ∎

E.J. CAMP—CORBIS OUTLINE (2)

JUNG: Avon is finally calling on a lady for leadership

FALLEN ARCHES: A besieged French franchise

CLAUDE PARIS—AP

First, Launder the Money

Forget Austin Powers: Martin Frankel was 1999's International Man of Mystery, a financial villain whose outsize chicanery and super-size embezzlement proved a match for our gaudy times. Frankel, 44,

Frankel

a.k.a. David Rosse, a.k.a. Eric Stevens, was accused of absconding with more than $200 million through a bewildering web of insurance companies, bogus investment funds and phony charitable organizations. By the time police and fire fighters responded to an alarm at his arcadian Greenwich, Conn., mansion in June, all they found was smoldering file cabinets full of incinerated incriminating documents: the perp had fled the coop. (Item No. 1 on his to-do list: launder money.) After a manhunt spanning 115 countries, Frankel was nabbed by German police at a hotel in Hamburg in September, with Cindy Allison, 35, a.k.a. Susan Kelley, at his side. They were watching the video of *Patch Adams* for the fifth time. Now *that's* evil.

Frankenfries–*Non*!

Poor Ronald McDonald. It was hard to visit a McDonald's anywhere in France in the fall without encountering mountains of fresh manure—as well as not-so-fresh fruit and vegetables—dumped in front of the restaurants by protesting farmers.

In part, their anger reflected increasing anxiety over genetically modified food, branded "Frankenfood" by critics. In the U.S., a group of 20 Congressmen introduced legislation that would require labeling of all genetically engineered food, which includes half of all soybeans, about a third of the corn crop and many of the potatoes grown in America.

Revenge of the Car Czars

For all their image as the caviar of automobile brands, Mercedes-Benz and Jaguar spent much of the '90s longing for a little meat-and-potatoes appeal. Stuffy images and the rising popularity of Japanese newcomer Lexus led to slumping sales in the U.S. for the haughty Germans and the aristocratic Brits. In 1999 both companies loosened up their styles. Mercedes rolled out a variety of elegant new sedans and sport-utility vehicles, and Jaguar was hoping its snazzy new S-class model—and a "Baby Jag" promised for 2000—would multiply global sales in two years.

People

Makeover for a Mogul

It was a very good year for Rupert Murdoch, reaching a high point when the billionaire media magnate, 68, married a former employee, Wendi Deng, 32, aboard his yacht in New York Harbor. It was Murdoch's third marriage, and he sprouted new wings after the ceremony, adopting the wardrobe of a beatnik and the eating habits of a monk. Murdoch told *Vanity Fair* magazine that his updated look, featuring lots of black, was due less to his new wife than to his sons. "I wanted to look like them," he said. "Forty years younger." Thus, he was visiting "some institute at UCLA—

TOM ROLLO—REUTERS-ARCHIVE

NEWLYWEDS: Deng and Murdoch

they've got me on a morning drink [of] fruit and soy powder," and working with a trainer who, he claimed, "tortures me for an hour every morning."

Not all was torture for Murdoch: his far-flung News Corp. was the world's most truly global media empire. With satellites hovering practically everywhere, he penetrated markets around the world. And his movie studio was hot, even if two of his U.S. toys, the Fox TV network and the L.A. Dodgers, were slumping.

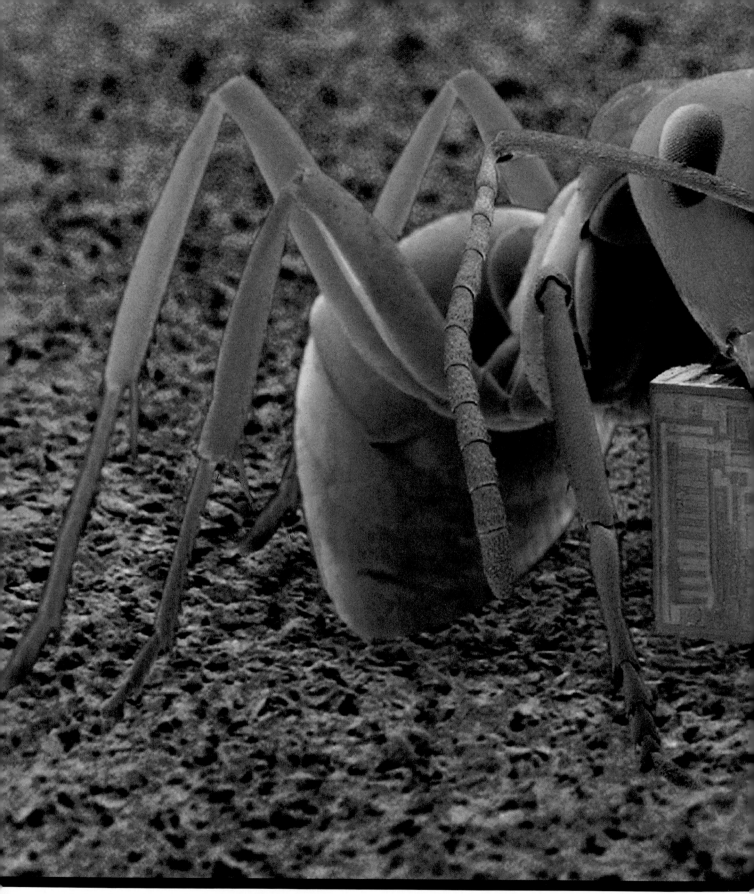

Andrew Syred—Science Photo Library–Photo Researchers

Even as microchips, cell phones and portable computers kept getting smaller, their impact kept getting larger. Digital technology was the motor driving change throughout society—in the way people worked, played, met, shopped, communicated. While Amazon, Yahoo! and eBay became familiar brand names, downloadable music technologies promised to reshape an entire industry.

SIZE DOES MATTER: In this scanning electron-microscope view, a woodland ant holds a microchip in its mouthparts.

Technology

BATTER UP! Justin Frankel's stats: 21 years old, $70 million in the bank. Any questions?

DISABLING THE SYSTEM

How a college dropout set out to make his computer play tunes better—and just about destroyed the music biz

RED-HAIRED JUSTIN FRANKEL, A BIG-BONED, GANGLY kid, is cranking out code in warp mode. It's 1995, and the high school sophomore is sprinting through a programming contest at the University of Northern Arizona. Frankel, 16, is so far ahead of his nearest competitor that, just for yucks, he decides to write a little "fork bomb"—a program that splits itself repeatedly until it swamps a computer system. He uploads it, and one by one, the machines around him crash. As administrators scramble, he sits in guilty silence, then finally confesses to a frazzled systems engineer.

Frankel wins anyway. The following year, the contest administrator warns students that foul play will not be tolerated. Looking straight into Frankel's eyes, she underlines her point. "No disabling the system," she says.

Luckily, in the intervening years Frankel has paid little attention to that bit of follow-the-leader advice. He set out to do another bit of creative programming, a piece of software called Winamp, which may just singlehandedly disable a $12 billion-a-year system—the music industry. He created his own company around Winamp, and in the summer of 1999 he sold the business (and perhaps himself) to America Online. Justin Frankel, disabler of systems, is currently worth $70 million. He turned 21 in October 1999.

You have to go back to 1987 to pinpoint the event that would change everything in the music industry. That's when the German engineering firm Fraunhofer Schaltungen devised a compression standard known as MPEG-1 Audio Layer 3, better known as MP3. The Germans were trying to solve a vexing problem: how to broadcast digital audio. CD-quality sound files were just too big and cumbersome. Fraunhofer Schaltungen figured out that you could compress the files in a way that eliminated the extraneous noise, but in those days of molasses-slow modems and processors, nobody thought this meant anything to PC users. Apply a few iterations of Moore's law, throw in T1 lines and cable modems, and MP3 suddenly caught on big in the mid-'90s with college students and tune-hungry techies. It became the de facto standard for "ripping" CDs: You could take a music disc and translate the songs into MP3, squeezing them down to a tenth of their uncompressed size—small enough to pass around on the Net.

But before that could happen, people needed a better way to listen to MP3s on their PCs. The software players available then used clunky Unix or Windows interfaces without personality. At least that's what Frankel thought during his two semesters at the University of Utah. While there, he hardly left his 8-ft. by 12-ft. room, hacking away on a Pentium 133 machine, eating too many Taco Bell Burrito Supremes—and ripping, uploading, downloading and listening to MP3s. When he quit school, complaining of boredom and missing his family, and returned home to Sedona, Ariz., it was MP3s that consumed him.

"I needed a better player," Frankel says. He wanted to build one that would look as familiar as a home stereo, with the sound quality jacked up with effects like 3-D surround sound. He also wanted a feature that allowed you to sort MP3 tracks or play them randomly the way a jukebox does. So he spent his days with his feet propped up on a subwoofer, interrupted every now and then by his mother, popping her head in to suggest it might be a good idea to go outside. "I was, like, 'Outside's overrated,'" he says. In April 1997, Winamp 1.0 was born.

A near perfect piece of consumer software, it had the same effect on the world of digital music that a 1994

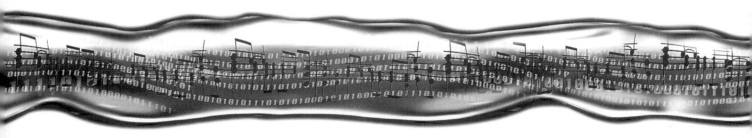

browser called Mosaic had on the world of the Internet and computing. It was the killer app, the Thing That Changed Everything. Within a month after Frankel uploaded the software for distribution from his website, it was getting 40,000 visitors a day. Within 18 months, the free Winamp program had been downloaded 15 million times.

"You rarely find the alpha geek who has the creative and technical skills to take a product singlehandedly from concept to an audience of 15 million users," says Rob Lord, Frankel's director of online strategies. The sheer volume meant that even the small percentage of users who sent in the suggested $10 registration fee amounted to a viable revenue stream. Sure enough, the traffic flowing into winamp.com was soon generating $8,000 a month in advertising fees alone. Frankel built a company, Nullsoft—the name was a gibe at Microsoft—around the product and hired half a dozen fellow twentysomethings to run the website and maintain the database of users. His father Charles, a lawyer, signed on as legal counsel and resident adult.

COLLEGE KIDS GOBBLED UP WINAMP. ONE FEATURE allowed users to make their own "skins"—snazzy wrappers for the player so it could take on the look of anything from Daisy Duke to Marilyn Monroe—which increased its exponential growth. Naturally, the trading of MP3s skyrocketed, since people wanted stuff to play in their cool Winamps—much to the distress of record companies, which suddenly saw more piracy than the Spanish Main.

An entire generation of college students now believes music is a free medium. Today's 20-to-24-year-olds are buying a third less music than the same age group 10 years ago, says the Record Industry Association of America. Hyped by the press and endorsed by musicians who feel stuck in unfair contracts with greedy record-industry moguls, MP3 has emerged as a kind of postpunk coolness indicator. On college campuses that offer T1 lines, as many as 75% of students have engaged in music piracy. "The Internet has made music so vulnerable," says RIAA general counsel Cary Sherman, "[that] if it were left unchecked, you would eventually reach a point where the pirate market would supplant the real market."

Ah, but until very recently there was no real market online. The MP3 boom thrived in a capitalist vacuum, with no competition from the forces of free trade. Yet thanks to Frankel, Winamp and all the other MP3 players that have come along, the music industry has suddenly been forced to retool its entire business—and compete.

■ HOW THE MUSIC BUSINESS HAS BEEN CHANGED

Yesterday: Flawed copies

For years, music was recorded primarily in analog format, using a microphone to convert sound waves into electrical pulses

Analog wave

Today: Perfect copies

Most music is recorded in a digital format, using computers to convert sound waves into a series of binary digits (0s and 1s)

Binary code
01010
01010
01010
01010

Tomorrow: Limited copies

An agreement reached in the summer mandates that additional code, known as a digital watermark, be invisibly blended into all copyrighted music

Encrypted co
010101
010100
001100
010101

That's why the Wild West days of Justin Frankel and MP3 may be coming to a close. The music industry first tried to stop the onslaught of digitally downloadable music by sweeping the Net for pirate sites and filing suit against hardware manufacturers like Diamond Multimedia, but now it's singing a different tune. It sees digital music as the next great revenue stream—maybe clearing $4 billion a year by 2004, according to Forrester Research. By the end of 1999, music was available for sale online from many major labels. Sony Music began releasing singles on its website in the summer. At the same time, a new generation of portable MP3 players was flooding the market.

The biggest change came in August, when the consortium of technology companies and record labels that make up the Secure Digital Music Initiative (SDMI) agreed on what executive director Leonardo Chiariglione called "a framework where different security solutions can be plugged in and provide a high degree of interoperability."

But how? Basic security—like watermarks encrypted into the music itself—can make casual piracy difficult. Yet

Hyped by the press and endorsed by musicians who hate the "greedy" record

The pulses are recorded as tiny magnetic patterns on a strip of tape

But the magnetic patterns are altered with each duplication, degrading the sound quality

COPY 1 COPY 2 COPY 3

The digits are then recorded as tiny pits on a CD and read by a laser

The data, on disc or converted to near CD quality in MP3 format, can be copied freely without losing fidelity

COPY 1 COPY 2 COPY 3
CD-R CD-R CD-R

0101010101010 0101010101010 0101010101010
0101010100101 0101010100101 0101010100101
0010101010100 0010101010100 0010101010100

The code would be hidden on every disc and on every song that can be downloaded

MP3 (or its successor)

When recording devices detect the code they will limit the number of copies that could be made

MP3 COPY 1 MP3 COPY 2
CD-R CD-R

0101010101010 0101010101010 0101010101010
0101011001100 0101011001100 0101011001100
1100111010100 1100111010100 1100111010100

CORBIS—AFP

as Lucas Graves, senior analyst at Jupiter Communications points out, "They [the record companies] will never eliminate piracy. What they can do is limit the casual ability to make copies and set up a legitimate system that is easy for the consumer."

In the meantime, record labels are scrambling to secure formats, software and distribution. Universal has aligned itself with AT&T, Matsushita and BMG to develop a shared codec, a compressor/decompressor, to allow digital transfer. Universal has also teamed up with InterTrust Technologies to develop digital-rights-management software. Universal's competitors are keeping pace. Sony and EMI are partnering with Microsoft, and Warner Music is teaming up with RealNetworks to digitize its catalog. In the short term, competing formats will make life confusing for consumers: not all players will play files from all codecs.

And Frankel? Not long after he joined AOL, there already were signs of the online giant's new dominion over Nullsoft—the most ominous being its blackout of a Shoutcast stream in June that was broadcasting hacked cellular-phone calls. Shoutcast is a streaming-audio product developed by Nullsoft that allows anyone with the Winamp plug-in to broadcast on the Net as if by ham radio. It has become wildly popular among young would-be deejays. Once upon a time, Frankel would have relished the dark-side cool of that kind of hacking. Now he has no choice but to go along with AOL's more civic-minded standards.

For the erstwhile hacker is now riding a desk at AOL, keeper of the Internet's sane middle ground. In a funny kind of way, his journey from the Internet's underground to its mainstream parallels the evolution of the online music business. Both started in the hacker counterculture and were absorbed by a music industry eager to cash in on a new distribution channel. Frankel's journey may be more a sign of where the digital-music scene is heading than any record-label initiatives or new compression algorithms. Yet he is uneasy about his new role—and that suggests that the struggle between this new frontier's outlaws and its businessmen is far from over. Watch out, AOL—your system may be the next to be disabled. ∎

companies, MP3 has emerged as a kind of 1990s postpunk coolness indicator

COOLEST GEAR OF THE YEAR

As the Age of the Geek begets hardware overload, you can't see the gadgets for the gizmos. Here's our pick of 1999's best

ALL RIGHT, SO THE HOTTEST NEW MACHINES OF 1999 MAY NOT HAVE BEEN exactly what we expected 20 or 30 years ago. We're still sadly lacking in flying cars, robot servants and that weird moon shuttle that used to show up in the last days of *Dick Tracy*. But take a peek at our personal spaces—our dens, shoulder bags, jacket pockets—and you'll know the end of the 2nd millennium did not lack for way-cool gadgets. Instead of kicking around at some dusty lunar motel, it seems, some of us wanted to play photo-realistic football in our pajamas. Or download CD-quality music from garage bands around the world, then listen to it on the subway. Or watch our favorite sitcoms without the incessant, annoying commercial breaks.

There are no one-size-fits-all innovations in end-of-the-century technology, so if you don't agree with TIME DIGITAL's pick for Machine of the Year—it's a video-game player, after all!—check out the runners-up. Because in our gizmo-hungry world, you can always choose something you like better. After all, though we haven't yet perfected the flying robot moon car, 1999 was the year when you could purchase the world's first robot dog, Sony's AIBO. This mechanical mutt had a camera in his nose, walked on all fours, wagged his tail and could get to his feet after lying on his back—another giant leap for robot-dog-kind. ∎

iBOOK Apple's "iMac to go," modeled at left by Steve Jobs, may do for the portable market what iMac did for the desktop—sell like crazy and leave the rest of the industry playing catch-up. The iBook morphs iMac's elegant, curvilinear design and Life Savers colors into an affordable portable with a bunch of minor innovations and one major one: AirPort, a PC version of the cordless phone. This $400 option allows up to 10 users to swap data and surf the Web wirelessly from as much as 150 ft. away.

MP3 PLAYERS The first portable MP3 player, Diamond Multimedia's Rio, kicked off a digital, downloadable, free-music revolution in 1998. When the second wave of players arrived in '99, the big guys were getting in on the action, as with Sony's Memory Stick Walkman.

NEW CELL PHONES Still think cell phones are for talking? Those of the next generation, now on sale, use digital signals—and allow for retrieving e-mail, Web browsing, two-way text messaging and dialing by voice command. And you can still call and say "Hi" to your robot dog.

Gadgets galore: to play music, play games—and play havoc with ads on TV

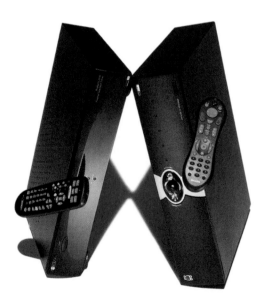

PERSONAL VIDEO RECORDERS
Easy-to-program PVRs save television shows to internal hard drives. Result: TV on demand. You can rewind or pause in the middle of a broadcast while still recording it, or flash past local car-lot commercials at superhigh speed.

SEGA DREAMCAST TIME DIGITAL's pick for Machine of the Year is the surprise-hit games console that is the first non-PC device that also gets you online at 56K speed—at a cost of less than $200. The cheap twofer vaulted slumping Sega past rivals Nintendo and Sony.

JOBS: TED THAI FOR TIME. CELL PHONES: URBANO DELVALLE FOR TIME. OTHER PHOTOS: TAKA FOR TIME DIGITAL

Source:
Tom Downes
and Shane
Greenstein

Distribution of
Internet-Service
Providers,
Oct. 1998

Over 10
4 to 10
1 to 3
0

The Plugged and the Un-Plugged

Got Net? Access to the Web turns America into a house divided—by bandwidth

WILEY MIDDLETON IS EXACTLY THE SORT OF FELLOW whom small towns love to welcome back home. A 45-year-old graphics designer who honed his craft in bigger cities, Middleton moved back to his native Leadville, Colo., in 1997, eager to enjoy the serenity of this historic mining town of 3,421. But Leadville's telephone system is quaint too, and won't let his computer modem send the digital images that are his livelihood. This regularly forces Middleton to drive two hours to Denver to deliver electronic designs for brochures and ads. "I can't compete," he laments. "The phone line is too small."

Or too narrow, to be more precise. Middleton's problem involves bandwidth, the amount of information his connection to the Internet can carry. Much of the country has moved up to 56K modems or adopted one of the new broadband telephone and cable-company services that offer the Net many times faster. But the aging patchwork of thin wires and microwave towers that brings phone service to remote spots like mountainous Leadville transmits at speeds of 28.8 kilobits per second or less. And the gap between online haves and have-nots is widening.

Many of the start-up businesses that are driving employment and wealth in the new economy are built around the Internet and won't locate where it can't be speedily accessed. Even established businesses require high-speed Net connections to communicate effectively with customers, suppliers and employees. Professionals consider the bandwidth available in a locality when they decide where to work, live and buy vacation homes. So do affluent retirees who track investments online. At the same time, kids who aren't skilled on the Net face a growing disadvantage in college and the job market.

Dead zones in cyberspace can be found in states like Georgia, Mississippi and Maine, but the digital divide is particularly acute in Western states. Consider that in New Jersey the average distance between a customer and the phone company's nearest switching facility is about 2.6 miles. In Wyoming the distance is twice as far, and the cost

In a nation that measures status by modem speed, geography is destiny

to the phone company of reaching a customer is twice as high, according to figures from Sprint.

A number of small towns are forging their own links to the Net. Some are forming cooperatives to string their own wire. Others are pulling strings. In Lusk, Wyo., a visionary mayor was able to get fiber-optic cable laid into his town of 1,600 and give its two schools access to a T1 line. Town leaders see it as a matter of survival. "We want our kids to come back here," says Twila Barnette of the county Chamber of Commerce. "But we have to be able to offer them opportunities using this new technology." ∎

ILLUSTRATION FOR TIME BY S.B. WHITEHEAD

Whee! A Gas-Free Lee!

He may be living in California, in exile from Detroit, but Lee Iacocca, father of the Mustang and the minivan, was alive and well at 75. Which is to say he was talking big again, this time about the kind of vehicle only a fully California-ized entrepreneur would attempt: an electric bicycle. "I spent all my life putting minivans and Jeeps in American garages," he says. "I think I have one vision left in me before I die, and it's electric." His EV Global Motors (as in, Electric Vehicle) began distributing the Taiwan-produced E-Bike in February. Fine, but a bicycle in the land of muscle cars? Keep in mind that Iacocca made his career betting against the short-term odds. And there has never been as much global political pressure to produce vehicles that don't pollute. In Asia and Europe, where noisy, gas-powered scooters are fast being outlawed, the electric-bike market is hot. "Why does a girl need a 4WD sport-utility vehicle in Beverly Hills?" said Lee. Hmmm ... maybe he *is* aging!

ART STREIBER—ICON INTERNATIONAL FOR TIME

Hey, Buddy! Can I Play?

Getting in touch with a friend? Thanks to instant messaging and the in-your-face presence of its address book (the "buddy list") on computer desktops, you can enjoy real-time chat with friends, family or co-workers who are online. In fact, instant messaging, or IM, now handles more missives each day than the U.S. Postal Service; analysts say it's the second most valuable piece of digital real estate in the world, after the Windows desktop. America Online, with 40 million folks using its free software, is the undisputed king of IM. But in mid-July, Microsoft tried to muscle in (surprise!), launching Microsoft MSN Messenger, which allowed AOL buddy-list users to sign in too—if they entered their password. That set off alarm bells at AOL, which promptly blocked Microsoft's access to its server. So Microsoft came up with a fix, which AOL also jammed. The cat-and-mouse game ended in mid-November when Microsoft backed down, restricting Messenger to MSN users only.

Virus of the Year: Melissa

Experts had never seen a computer virus spread so fast. Everyone trusted Melissa, who arrived disguised as an e-mail from a friend.

Soon she was replicating herself all over cyberspace, shutting down more than 300 computer networks. That called for a virtual manhunt. Thanks to the imaginative sleuthing team of Fredrik Bjorck, a computer-science grad student in Sweden and Richard M. Smith, below right,

BROOKS KRAFT—CORBIS SYGMA FOR TIME

VIRUS HUNT: A tale of two Smiths

president of Phar Lap Software in Massachusetts, a suspect was arrested only a week after allegedly releasing his corrupting creation. Charged: David L. Smith, on left above, 30, a resident of New Jersey.

>>> DUBBING: A GLOSSARY OF VALLEYSPEAK <<<

Tired of coming off as a clueless newbie around your Internet gazillionaire friends? Try this glossary of Silicon Valley babble:

CLICKS AND MORTAR A bricks-and-mortar company that makes the decision to go online

DUB-DUB-DUB Short for WWW

OPM Other people's money (so you needn't worry about failure)

OPEN THE KIMONO Reveal your business plan to another person

PLANE MONEY Signing bonus for execs; sometimes these can be enough to buy a private plane

X Times as big. As in: "We're going to be Amazon.com 3X."

YACC Yet another calendar company; an overused idea

Steve Liss

More than ever, American society seemed to be vibrating to a digital impulse: some families were tracing their roots online; some were tracking the peaks and valleys of tech stocks. Still others were hunkering down, waiting for the predicted Y2K disaster that they seemed in part to fear—and in part to crave.

BE PREPARED: In Arkansas, Jerry and Carolyn Head show off some of the stockpile they gathered in preparation for a Y2K computer meltdown.

Society

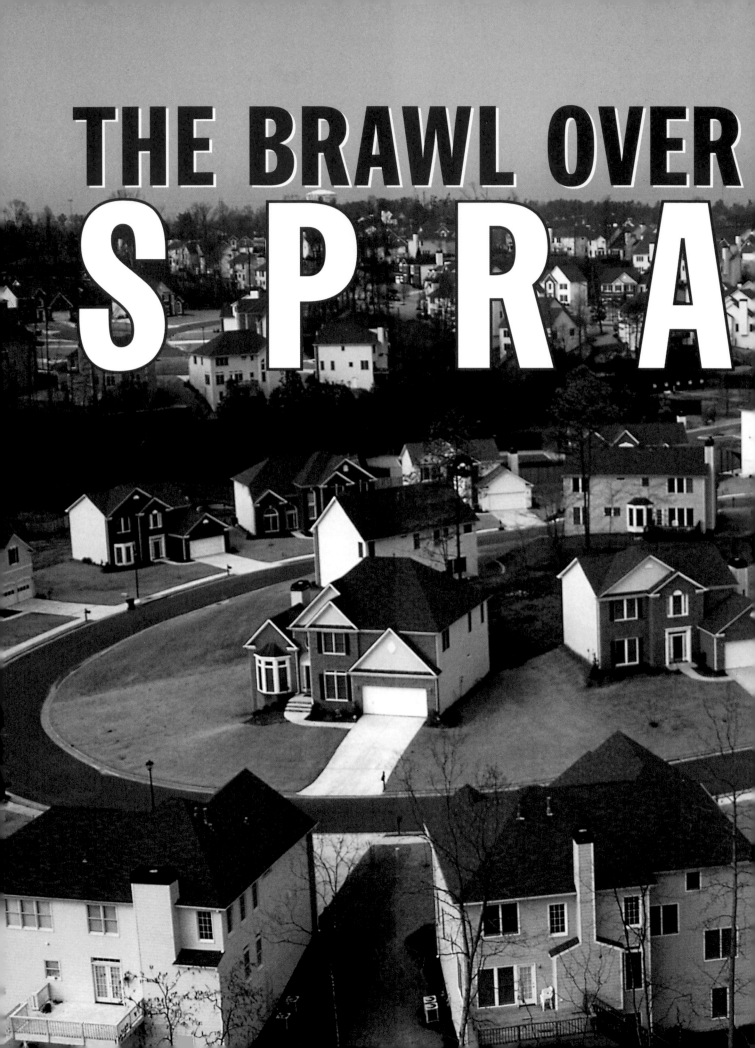

THE BRAWL OVER
SPRA

GEORGIA

INSTANT CITY: New homes are planted in Gwinnett County, part of greater Atlanta's 13-county explosion

From strip mall to shining strip mall, Americans fight an encircling tide of dreary, paved-over subdivisions

TRUST RALPH WALDO EMERSON TO PEER INTO THE future. In 1842 he wrote, "Whew! Whew! Whew! How is real estate here in the swamp and wilderness?" And he'd never even seen a strip mall. Which brings us to greater Atlanta, 1999. Once a wilderness, it's now a 13-county eruption, one that has been called the fastest-spreading human settlement in history. Already more than 110 miles across, up from just 65 in 1990, it consumes an additional 500 acres of field and farmland every week. What it leaves behind is tract houses, access roads, malls, off ramps, industrial parks and billboards advertising more tract houses where the peach trees used to be. Car exhaust is such a problem that Washington is withholding new highway funding until the region complies with federal clean-air standards. On a bad traffic day—basically any weekday with a morning and evening in it—you can review whole years of your life in the time it takes to get from Blockbuster to Fuddruckers.

"We can't go on like this," says Georgia Governor Roy Barnes, a "smart growth" Democrat who was elected in 1988. Barnes has proposed a regional transportation authority that can block local plans for the new roads that encourage development. But dumb growth is not confined to Atlanta. Half a century after America loaded the car and fled to the suburbs, these boundless, slapdash places are making people want to flee once more.

Whew! Suburban overgrowth has become a national headache. But now, instead of just fleeing the sprawl (and thus creating more of it), people are groping for ways to fight it. In 1998 there were no fewer than 240 antisprawl ballot initiatives around the country. Most of them passed. Some stripped local authorities of the power to approve new subdivisions without voter assent. Others okayed tax money to buy open land before developers do. In the largest of those, New Jersey Governor Christine Whitman successfully pushed a referendum to use sales-tax money to buy half the state's undeveloped land—a million acres.

Twelve states have enacted growth-management laws. Tennessee has one of the strictest, requiring many cities to impose growth boundaries around their perimeters. In Maryland, counties get state money for roads and schools only if they agree to confine growth to areas that the state has designated as suitable. But managed growth is not a win-win proposition. When laws make it harder to build in the countryside, new development is pressed into more expensive land closer to town. That can mean higher home prices, so a couple who make $38,000 a year must choose between a tiny apartment close to work and a 90-minute commute to housing they can afford.

Limiting growth also means dealing with a profound conflict between the good of the community and the rights of the individual. For a lot of people, the good life still means a big house with a big yard. Who's to say they shouldn't get

it? Yet smart growth envisions a nation packaged into town houses and small apartments, whose citizens ride trains and buses and leave the car at home. Everybody hates the drive time, the scuffed and dented banality, of overextended suburbs. But how many Americans are prepared to embrace the confinement and compromise the solutions will require? A spring '99 TIME/CNN poll showed that most people like greenbelts but don't trust government planning.

If America's mushrooming metro regions were caused by population growth alone, sprawl would be inescapable. But they are equally the result of political decisions and economic incentives that lure people ever farther from center cities. For decades, federal highway subsidies have paid for the roads to those far-flung malls and tract houses. Then there are local zoning rules that require large building lots, ensuring more sprawl. Many localities fiercely resist denser housing because it brings in more people but less property-tax revenue. Zoning rules commonly forbid any mix of homes and shops, which worsens traffic by guaranteeing that you burn a quart of gas to find a quart of milk. Even more important, localities routinely agree to ex-

Everybody hates the drive time, the scuffed and dented banality, of overextendeo

Americans do believe in property rights—including the right to profit by selling. So the farmers and ranchers who feel squeezed out when tract housing plunks down next to their pasture often think about cashing in. One way to solve the problem, being used in parts of Colorado, is "development rights," which let builders put up houses more densely near town in exchange for payments to outlying farmers and ranchers to keep land open.

There's another option being explored in Ventura County, northwest of Los Angeles. At night, once dark hillsides are strung with lights from new tract housing. Those twinkling lights worked on Steve Bennett, a soft-spoken high school history teacher, until he'd had enough. Three years ago he co-founded SOAR (Save Open Space and Agricultural Resources) to get antisprawl initiatives on the ballot. It took just nine weeks last year for Bennett and his allies to collect the 75,000 signatures they needed. In November 1988, large majorities in four of Ventura's five largest cities adopted rules that forbid the county to rezone land for development without voter approval. A fifth city came on board in January.

But a local farmers' organization fought the SOAR measure. Why? An appraisal by the city of Ventura concluded that 87 acres would be worth $1.6 million as farmland but $13 million if zoned for development. "The people of this county have taken away my property rights," says Howard Atkinson, 51, who inherited part of a 57-acre ranch.

tend roads, sewer lines and other utilities to new suburban developments, while existing schools and housing stock are left to decay. Yet "impact fees" on developers cover just a fraction of these services actually cost.

These incentives to expand help create cities that widen much faster than their populations grow. Between 1990 and 1996, metro Kansas City spread 70%, while its population, now 1.9 million, increased just 5%. In that period greater Portland, Ore., spread just 13%, the same growth rate as its population, now 1.7 million. Portland has long been the laboratory city for smart growth. In 1979, as part of its compliance with a groundbreaking statewide land-use law, Portland imposed a "growth boundary," a ring enclosing the city proper and 23 surrounding towns.

1973
GROWING: A view of bucolic Moorpark, Calif.

1986
GROWING: The valley's new roads and tract housing shoulder aside farmland

Within that circle, the Portland-area metro council, the only directly elected regional government in the U.S., controls all development. Inside, permits for new construction are granted readily, which helps account for the construction cranes all around a downtown that looked ready to die 20 years ago. Outside, where open land is strictly protected, there's mostly just the uninterrupted flight of greenery we call nature. Unspoiled stretches of the Willamette River Valley start 15 miles from city hall.

Orderly growth comes at a price. Smaller towns within the ring are submerged by crowding they might otherwise zone out. And within the dwindling buildable space of the ring, the average lot size has shrunk almost by half

suburbs. But are we ready for the alternative?

over the past 20 years. Yet the median price of a single-family home has more than doubled in just 10 years, from $64,000 to $159,900. Once among the most affordable American cities for housing, Portland has now become the third most expensive, slightly cheaper than San Francisco.

VIRGINIA

STARTING OVER: Tired of being only an "edge city," Tysons Corner is building a town center to foster civic identity

Keeping land open is only half the battle. The other half is keeping downtowns livable and affordable so people stay happily bunched there. But for the centerless "edge cities" that collect around major highways, the problem is to create a downtown where none has existed before. That's the challenge facing Tysons Corner, Va., just outside Washington, D.C., where county officials in 1999 put the stamp of approval on an instant town center—an 18-acre collection of small office buildings that will also house shops and restaurants around a plaza.

The revival of downtowns in places like San Diego and Denver—and, for that matter, Atlanta—and the reaction against sprawl among the suburbanites who spawned it may be signs that the problem can be fixed. But sprawl is mostly indelible ink. Once the roads and houses and strip malls set in, you can't just get them out. The best way to fight sprawl is to stop it before it starts. ∎

1999

GONE: Fed-up voters in five towns of Ventura County stripped officials of the power to approve development without their assent

"PLEASE, WILL SOMEBODY HELP ME? I'M NEW AT this, and I have no idea what I'm doing." Those words were not some perverse message smeared in lipstick across a rest-room mirror. They were posted on the volunteers' bulletin board of America Online's genealogy site, typed by G. Marie Leaner, a communications consultant in Chicago, looking for her family roots.

Leaner's plaintive cry was heard by a volunteer researcher who told Leaner about the Social Security Death Index. That was the breakthrough Leaner needed, allowing her to move out onto the Internet and into libraries, gathering snippets about her heritage. Now, thanks to scores of websites and chat groups, she has traced her great-great-grandparents back to Mississippi, found the cemetery in Hines County where they are buried, obtained a copy of their 1874 marriage license—along with the World War I draft card of a great-grandfather—and in the process, discovered the thrill of cyberrooting. "It's kind of spooky," she says. "Whenever I come upon something, my heart starts racing."

Once a hobby practiced mainly by self-satisfied blue bloods tracing their families back to the *Mayflower*, genealogy is fast becoming a national obsession—for new parents basking in the glow of family life, baby boomers wrestling with their first intimations of mortality, and var-

Be forewarned: much of what is on the Web now is akin to signposts—lists of documents but rarely the documents themselves. The National Archives provides a description of its material online—but only 120,000 of its 4 billion records have been digitized. Much of the Net's information is posted by volunteers who transcribe cemetery headstones or newspaper obituaries—with predictable human error. Most serious researchers argue that only an exact copy of an original marriage certificate or immigration visa can be trusted.

Starting to get interested? If you remain willing to forgo leisurely weekends for a search that is bound to be alternately tedious and exhilarating, here's how:

STARTING UP. Whether you read a how-to book, click on a website with beginner's tips, take a course on family-history research or join a genealogical club, you must first decide on a collection system. You can use note cards, three-ring binders or software, but each new twig on the family tree must be documented, with notes on its source. That's why computers, which can organize massive amounts of data, are ideal. Remember that for each generation back, the number of parents doubles; by the time you hit 20 generations, it's up to more than 1 million.

If you're computer phobic, rest assured: you can do without. Working with a vintage Smith-Corona, Ida Quin-

Ancestors Online

Americans are using the vast resources of the Web to trace their family trees

ious ethnic groups exploring their pride and place in a multicultural society. Powering the phenomenon are the new tools of the digital age: computer programs that turn the search for family trees into an addiction; websites that make it easy to find and share information; and chat rooms filled with folks seeking advice, swapping leads, even sharing old photos and documents. "The Internet has helped democratize genealogy," says Stephen Kyner, editor of *The Computer Genealogist* magazine.

Roots seeking ranks with sex, finance and sports as a leading subject on the Internet. In March 1999 more than 160 million messages made their way through RootsWeb (*www.rootsweb.com*), a vast electronic trading post for genealogical information, and the three top genealogy websites had an audience of 1.3 million individual devotees.

But genealogy, as any veteran will tell you, is no cushy computer-desk job. Its aficionados are besieging county historical societies, rummaging through newspapers' microfilm, tramping through rural courthouses and overgrown cemeteries. Each year 800,000 people visit the Mormons' Family History Library in Salt Lake City. Officially known as the Church of Jesus Christ of Latter-Day Saints, the Mormons consider genealogy part of their mission and have the world's most extensive records.

tana Foraci, 70, explored her family, discovered a French-speaking Pawnee grandmother and traced her ancestors through families intertwined since New Mexico was part of Spain. She delved into archdiocesan records, statistical abstracts and old Spanish histories at the Denver Public Library. On a monthly pension of $400, she sold most of her furniture so she could publish her findings: 22 volumes that trace her history back to the arrival of conquistador Don Juan Onate in 1598. It is now a valuable resource for Hispanic genealogists. "I spent the past seven years looking," she says, "and I found me."

The first step is to write down everything you know about your family. Then interview relatives, oldest ones first. Videotape or tape-record them if possible. Ask for exact names, dates and places, and as many details of your ancestors' lives as they can remember. Copy all documents: birth, christening, marriage and death certificates, school and medical records, family-Bible inscriptions, military papers, old letters.

ROOTS SURFING. Genealogists disagree on whether to begin by searching the many rich websites devoted to genealogy or by traveling directly to a source for documents, whether it's the local branch of the National Archives, a well-stocked genealogical library such as the Newberry in Chicago or the Clayton in Houston. Often, the Web is a clear time saver. George Warholic, an economic consultant in Maryland, set out in 1983 to trace his Ukrainian relatives. "It was a chore," he remembers. "I spent weeks at the Library of Congress searching hundreds of telephone books for people with the same name. Now this information can be got in a few hours on the Internet."

DIGGING FOR DOCUMENTS. As you embark on your search, think of yourself as part historian, part detective. Federal records, vast and varied, can be researched at the National Archives and its 13 regional branches as well as at major libraries—and not necessarily online. Because of privacy laws, the U.S. Census is only made public after 72 years have passed since the time it was taken. Next to be opened is the 1930 census, which will become available in 2002. Early censuses, beginning in 1790, are sketchy, but by the mid-19th century they begin to be filled with rich detail, listing everyone in the family by name, age, occupation and place of birth. Starting with 1900, one can find out the

es sometimes read like whodunits. Wars and natural disasters wreak havoc: the U.S. 1890 Census was almost completely wiped out in a fire, and Southern courthouses were burned in the Civil War. The public records office in Dublin, Ireland, was destroyed in a fire in 1922. In China's Cultural Revolution, the centuries-old ancestor records compiled by villages were declared "feudal garbage."

Names, one discovers, can be tricky—even without adoptions, divorces and illegitimate children. Immigrants disembarking at Ellis Island found their names arbitrarily Anglicized. And some families, wanting to assimilate, did so later on their own. Jewish researchers run into a specific set of complications: traditionally Jews did not have surnames; they were called, for instance, Isaac, son of Jacob. Only beginning in the late 18th century were surnames imposed by edicts passed in Europe and Russia.

DEALING WITH SURPRISES. In a celebrity-obsessed culture, it is no wonder that some roots seekers hope to uncover an aristocratic connection. But just as often, skeletons emerge from

Digging up the past? Be prepared to haunt cemeteries, county courthouses, historical societies—and the local jail

year of immigration, whether English was spoken and whether a home was owned or rented.

Yet online genealogy information is a chaotic hodgepodge. The scope can be as broad as the U.S. Social Security Death Index, which draws on some 60 million records of those for whom a lump-sum death benefit was paid, mostly between 1963 and 1997; and as specific as the street maps of Eastern Europe on the Shtetlseeker page of the JewishGen website.

Federal records are rich troves for census, immigration and military records. Prison logs can be helpful too: "Pray that there were sinners in your family," says Denver Public Library genealogy specialist James Jeffrey. Try rooting in county courthouses and local historical societies for land deeds, wills and probate, and tax rolls. Local newspaper archives can tell you more than you want to know. Dennis Rawlings, a Fort Myers, Fla., real estate broker, unearthed an account of his great-grandparents' wedding in Cedar Bluffs, Neb. Guests were named, the bride's dress described and the presents included five pickle casters. "Pickle casters must have been the late-1800s equivalent of can openers," he jokes.

OVERCOMING OBSTACLES. Roots seeking inevitably demands patience—and ingenuity. Genealogists' obstacle cours-

the family closet. The International Black Sheep Society of Genealogists has set up a website and an electronic mailing list for "those who have a dastardly, infamous individual of public knowledge and ill repute in their family." The good news: roots seeking is healing old wounds. More and more, blacks and whites are cooperating in joint genealogy searches. Says Colorado land appraiser James Rogers, a Caucasian who unearthed a slave ancestor: "It certainly brought home to me that we are all related."

In the days when your relatives mostly stayed put, they knew more about one another's lives and deaths. But in today's mobile society, as nuclear families splinter, loneliness and alienation are the order of the day. "We are witnessing the atomization of the family," says David Altshuler, director of Manhattan's Museum of Jewish Heritage. "The coming of the millennium focuses people's attention on the disappearance of an era." That nostalgia, the sense of lost roots, has fired a thirst for connection that genealogy seems to satisfy. Middle-aged and older people, who form the majority of roots seekers, talk about leaving a legacy for their children—a family deeper and broader than ever imagined. For many Americans, that long journey begins with a single click of the mouse. ∎

ATTENTION! Near Fort Hood, a priestess leads soldiers in a Wiccan ritual

People

Shattering Stereotypes

Is Jerry Falwell mellowing with age? In late October, 200 of Falwell's supporters met with 200 gay people of faith, and the Christian conservative leader apologized for his harsh earlier stands against gays. Rev. Falwell agreed to break bread with the Christian gays after several talks with the Rev. Mel White, a 60-year-old gay activist who runs Soulforce, an ecumenical gay group. White and Falwell used to be pals; White, a former filmmaker and conservative writer, ghostwrote Falwell's autobiography. Tired of fighting his true nature and incensed by one of Falwell's gay-baiting fundraising pitches, White came out to Falwell late in 1991. "Homosexuals are the last pariahs in this society," Falwell said. "We've got to reach out."

"I Saluted a Witch"

You've heard of Army brats. Now meet the Army witches: colonels and sergeants and captains and privates, members of a group of 50 or so kindred spirits who assemble regularly at Fort Hood in Texas, the largest U.S. military base. They are part of a boomlet in the military of believers who call themselves Wiccans and follow a polytheistic, nature-based religion that centers on an earth goddess (no, not Madeleine Albright). Fort Hood gave official recognition to the Wiccans some years before, and since then four other military bases have sanctioned the religion.

Nobody much noticed—until a photo of a pagan torchlight ritual ran in a local newspaper. As word spread, Christian groups and politicians denounced the Wiccans as satanic and inappropriate in the U.S. Army. "What's next?" asked one G.O.P. legislator: "Will armored divisions be forced to travel with sacrificial animals for satanic rituals?" The Army, citing the First Amendment, said it had no plans to shut down "minority religions."

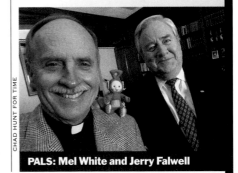

PALS: Mel White and Jerry Falwell

Terrified Tabloids Invaded by Alien Values!

The recipe for magazines in 1999: buzz and bimbos. Heading up the buzz-busters was Tina Brown, erstwhile *Vanity Fair* and *New Yorker* editor, who launched her monthly collaboration with the Miramax movie folks, *Talk*. By year's end, New York publishing circles were buzzing more about *Talk*'s masthead than its pages: four top editors had left in four months. Meanwhile, the smash British import *Maxim* led the bust-boosters, driving other men's magazines into a heightened fascination with all things bosomy. And who was left to defend decent journalistic values? Believe it or not: the supermarket

tabloids, the top three of which are all now owned by hard-driving exec David Pecker—the Bill Gates of the tabloid world. The new boss vowed he would remake his No. 1 *National Enquirer* and No. 2 *Star*, softening their famously antic stories by banishing alien babies and similar follies. Pecker was taking a real risk: Compared with classic headlines like KILLS PAL AND EATS PIECES OF HIS FLESH, new *Enquirer* banners like DEMI TO WED! seemed a wee bit pallid.

Doug Pensinger—Allsport

The bad news: a generation of authentic heroes—Jordan and Elway, Gretzky and Graf—left the field, and the Olympic rings were tarnished by revelations of corruption. The good news: a new wave of stars brought a fresh breeze into sports. Lance Armstrong scored a double triumph: first over cancer, then in the Tour de France. And Americans cheered a band of ponytailed heroines who won soccer's World Cup.

TRES CHIC! His yellow leader's jersey matching a field of summer flowers, Armstrong is well on the way to victory in cycling's most important event.

Sport

W E'VE ALREADY WON, NO MATTER WHAT THE score is going to be." Hank Steinbrecher, the general secretary of U.S. Soccer, was crowing even before the American team's draining, dramatic penalty-kick shoot-out win over China in the 1999 Women's World Cup. And win they did. When defender Brandi Chastain blasted the team's fifth penalty kick past Chinese goalkeeper Gao Hong after 120 scoreless minutes, including two overtime periods, she put a fitting exclamation point on a summer of soccer that had swept the nation off its feet.

This sweet, sweet victory was very much an act of faith—not the end of a game so much as of a crusade. The U.S. women were good, they were good looking, and they were on a mission to prove that women's team sports, and soccer in particular, deserve the same kind of attention, admiration and money that the guys get. "I grew up watching Magic Johnson and Kareem Abdul-Jabbar, men I could never emulate," says Julie Foudy, the thoughtful, funny midfielder who leads the team in quotes. "Girls need role models." The goal of the Women's World Cup is no less than the establishment of a women's professional league to create those role models, a strategy similar to one the men used to launch Major League Soccer after the successful 1994 Men's World Cup, also held in the U.S.

The final had a look that observers of the men's game found familiar: a taut, defensive contest that tightens leg

First on offense, first on defense and first in the hearts of their countrymen, the U.S. women are soccer's world . . .

CHAMPS!

PETER READ MILLER—SPORTS ILLUSTRATED

muscles, turns feet into anchors and transforms a 116-yd. by 72-yd. field into a postage stamp. At their own end, the Americans completely snuffed out the Chinese offense, allowing scoring star Sun Wen precious little room to maneuver. At midfield, Michelle Akers, a 33-year-old orthopedic disaster, made her last World Cup game a memorable one. On defense, she owned the air, hurling herself at anything round that moved—a recklessness that forced her out of the game near the end of regulation time, when she crashed into U.S. goalie Briana Scurry.

Late in a nerve-racking overtime, the U.S. pressed the Chinese defense, but it would not break, denying a frenzied crowd a sudden-death triumph. And China almost stole the match away minutes later, when Fan Yunjie's header off a corner kick was cleared by Kristine Lilly.

So the game went to a penalty-kick shoot-out, which soccer players dread. The pressure is enormous, the con-

A relative newcomer in a group that has played together for many years, goalie Briana Scurry is one of the team's anchors. Above, she makes the critical play in the final-match shoot-out. Anticipating the direction of the shot, Scurry stopped the penalty kick from China's Liu Ying to set up the game-winning score by defender Brandi Chastain. Scurry is still the American team's only black starter

Widely considered the sport's best player—she holds the world record for goals scored—Mia Hamm is a reluctant diva who puts the team first, even if she is on PEOPLE's most-beautiful list

Caught in a typical posture—soaring through space—Michele Akers is the team's oldest, toughest player, and "one of the greatest women athletes in history," says Coach Tony DiCicco

sequences huge and the shoot-out no real indicator that the best team won. But the shoot-out is soccer's tie breaker: 12 yards out, shooter against keeper, with the odds overwhelmingly against the keeper. That was true of the first four penalty kicks. On China's third shot, however, Scurry guessed left and threw herself in that direction, where she met Liu Ying's kick. "I just went totally on instinct," she said. "I knew if I could get one, it would be O.K." The crowd erupted and, after Lilly's left-footer beat Chinese goalie Gao, sensed something big was about to happen.

China's next two shooters, Zhang Ouying and Sun, calmly found their marks, leaving it all up to Chastain, who had committed a huge gaffe against Germany in the quarterfinals when she scored in her own net. This time she found the right one, prompting the spontaneous strip.

Even before Chastain's heroics, something magical had been brewing for this team as the tournament progressed. As the NHL and NBA playoffs came and went, this was the one sports story that continued to build like a thunderstorm. Four years ago in Sweden, the American

team was dismissed in the semifinals before a scant 3,000 souls. In the days before last year's final, nearly that many fans were showing up to watch the team practice, and the players needed police escorts to make their way off the field. Foudy described this spring's frenzied postgame autograph sessions as a "Beatles-concert-slash-slumber-party." Teenagers, boys and girls, besieged them, and several of the players told stories of girls' breaking into tears upon getting an autograph—or just getting near team members.

The first taste of glory came at Giants Stadium near New York City, where Mia Hamm helped hammer Denmark in a 3-0 win, opening the scoring with a terrific strike in the 17th minute. That was expected. What nobody expected, at least initially, was a crowd of 79,000 cheering fans. There were painted faces and flags and banners, and an entire section of fans wearing Kristine Lilly shirts. It looked as if someone had gone to suburban malls and parks and hijacked shoppers and picnickers to the stadium. The players were stunned, and after the game Hamm noted that even the usually voluble Foudy was speechless.

Reporters who wouldn't know an offside trap from a lobster pot were now descending on the team's lone media rep demanding exclusives. David Letterman pronounced himself "team owner" and began plugging away. Even Tom Brokaw went to the final game at Pasadena's Rose Bowl for an on-the-scene report.

THERE WERE PLENTY OF GOOD STORIES WAITING TO be discovered—"eight- or nine-year overnight sensations," said Nike president Thomas Clarke. After all, this was a veteran group whose members have known one another, and played together, for a decade in some cases. They won the Olympic gold medal in 1996, and some, including Akers, were around in 1991, when the team won the inaugural World Cup, held in China, where the event apparently was kept a state secret. Indeed, the team barely played the next year because U.S. Soccer couldn't afford to pay anyone.

Wherever the team went in those days, the hero whom girls sought out was Hamm, 27 in 1999, whose speed and finesse still give defenders the shakes. As the team's best-known player—a distaff version of Michael Jordan—she had the burden of not only scoring goals but also being Miss Publicity. A self-described emotional child from a military family who lost an older brother to a rare blood disease (and still wears his initials on her soccer shoes), Hamm found the soccer field a perfect outlet for her inner fire. She's been on the national team since she was 15.

For Akers, who preceded Hamm to stardom, this Cup was a test of willpower. Dogged by chronic fatigue syndrome and damaged knees, she pursued the Cup as relentlessly as she has tracked down opposing midfielders. With the Summer Olympics coming up in 2000, Akers has said she will listen to what her body is telling her about whether to play. That would be a first for someone whose body has been screaming at her for years.

Originally, tournament organizers figured Women's World Cup could sell a total of about 312,000 tickets for the 17 doubleheaders. Instead the figure topped 650,000. While professional women soccer players are no match for the men in skill levels, their game is great entertainment because unlike the final, most games are freewheeling shoot-outs. It was all scintillating soccer, blissfully devoid of drunks and hooligans—just hundreds of thousands of soccer-loving Americans out for good, clean fun.

Now that the American team has reclaimed the championship, however, there is business to take care of. This is sports, after all. The women are eager to get a pro league started, perhaps with some of the profits this tournament will have generated quite unexpectedly. And there is the matter of the players' contract with U.S. Soccer, which expires soon. Some team players earn less than $30,000—coffee money for a male professional. Says Steinbrecher, sounding like a negotiator: "We can't afford to pay them what we think they're worth." He may just have to try a little harder. Welcome to the big time, ladies. ∎

Forget the boors, the beers and the jeers: the women's team filled stadiums with painted, ponytailed partisans—plus assorted moms, dads and brothers

TORE BERGSAKER—CORBIS SYGMA

GO, U.S.A.! In a scene repeated across the country, fans at Pasadena's Rose Bowl get rowdy for Foudy and friends

Triumph and Tears

BINGO! Stewart
sinks a 15-footer to
win the U.S. Open
on the last hole

DAVID CANNON—ALLSPORT

A year of golf milestones ends with the sudden death of a popular champion

FOR LOVERS OF GOLF, 1999 WAS THE BEST OF TIMES AND the worst of times. Here was Tiger Woods, winning an unheard-of eight PGA tournaments and cementing his legend at the grand old age of 23. Here was the fresh face of Sergio Garcia, the engaging young Spaniard with the big smile who stole Americans' hearts with his gallant bid for the PGA crown. Here was a last-minute comeback by the U.S. in the Ryder Cup, one of the most dramatic victories the game has ever seen. Here was a spine-tingling finish by veteran Payne Stewart, rolling in a pressure putt on the 72nd hole to win the U.S. Open. And here we encounter the sad news that plunged the golf world into mourning: on Oct. 25, Stewart, 42, a favorite of galleries around the world, was lost in an eerie accident when the Learjet that was carrying the golfer, three of his associates and two pilots to one of the year's final tournaments unaccountably flew far off course and crashed in South Dakota.

With Stewart's death, the golf world lost an original. Wearing his distinctive plus-fours, tam and silver-tipped alligator shoes, the Springfield, Mo., native was one of the world's most recognizable golfers. He special-ordered the silk for his knickers from Italy and awoke early on the mornings of tournaments to press his colorful costume. But his game, and demeanor, hadn't really caught up to his fame until recently. Early in his career, Stewart's play was often erratic, marred by several final-round chokes. He could be cocky and abrasive.

Lately, though, he had matured and mellowed; in 1999 he won two tournaments for the first time since 1990. He

finished the year with eight tour victories, and nine worldwide, a number last matched by Johnny Miller in 1974. The $1 million Valderrama winner's check gave Woods a take of more than $6.6 million for the year, more than twice the previous record. Said the popular champion: "I don't know how much better I will get. But I will tell you one thing. I will continue to work hard."

If Tiger ever stops working hard and looks in the rearview mirror, he may just see someone coming up behind him. Sergio Garcia is a Tiger useta-be, a charismatic 19-year-old with a fast grin, faster club-head speed and a palpable love of the game and its lore. The son of a Spanish golf pro and a woman who worked in the clubhouse shop, Garcia was an unknown amateur in 1998. By the end of 1999, he was an idol at home and a phenomenon worldwide. Garcia nearly stole the PGA from Woods. Eyes closed, he slashed at a ball burrowed behind a tree, then sprinted up

WOW! The U.S. wins the Ryder Cup on Leonard's masterly putt

Garcia is a Tiger Woods useta-be, a charismatic 19-year-old with a fast grin, faster club-head speed and a palpable love for the game and its lore

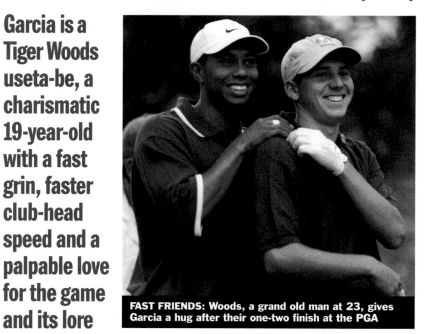

FAST FRIENDS: Woods, a grand old man at 23, gives Garcia a hug after their one-two finish at the PGA

ranked third among the Tour golfers in money won in 1999 and third in money won over a career. A diagnosis of attention-deficit disorder and sessions with a sports psychologist had helped Stewart's focus; he credited his family and a renewed sense of religion for his new steadiness.

The season-crowning Tour Championship, a prestigious showdown among an élite field, quickly became an impromptu Stewart memorial tourney. Play was canceled on the tournament's second day so the pros could attend a service for the Open champ. On the first day, 24 of 29 players wore plus-fours in his honor; in a moving moment, a bagpiper appeared out of the mist on the first fairway, offering a final, stately salute to the fallen star.

Stewart's death slightly obscured the remarkable run of Woods, who in 1999 surpassed all but the most extravagant predictions he had been saddled with over the years. Woods won the Tour Championship, and a week later he won the last event of the tour year, the American Express Championship at the Valderrama Golf Club in Spain. He

the fairway and leaped into the air to see the marvelous result. Despite his big finish, he came up one shot shy of the invincible Tiger—but wait till next year.

For big finishes, nothing could top September's Ryder Cup. The U.S. team under captain Ben Crenshaw had to win six of 12 matches and tie another on the final day to win—and they did it, capped by Justin Leonard's clutch 45-ft. putt on the 17th hole of his match with Spain's José Maria Olazabal. The event had been marred by the unruly behavior of some U.S. fans, who taunted the visitors in a manner more often found at the ballpark than the golf course. But Stewart put that right with a wonderful grace note at the conclusion of play. With the event already in the bag for the U.S., Britain's Colin Montgomerie faced a tough short putt to tie Stewart. But the American spared his foe. He walked over and picked up his opponent's ball—losing the now meaningless match but winning hearts everywhere with his deft feel for the game's heritage of sportsmanship. He will be missed. ∎

MCGWIRE: Sans muscle builders, he smacks 65 dingers

RYAN REMIORZ—AP; RON KUENSTLER—AP

SOSA: Once again Sammy was close—but no cigar

And Now, the Instant-Replay Season

Big Mac and Sammy duel, the Yankees rule—and all's right with the world

LET'S SEE IF WE'VE GOT THIS STRAIGHT. MARK MC GWIRE and Sammy Sosa are blitzing the fences of National League ballparks in a home-run duel that will see both shatter the old records of Babe Ruth and Roger Maris. The race goes right down to the wire, culminating when their St. Louis Cardinals and Chicago Cubs meet in the last series of the season. Meanwhile, over in the American League, the invincible New York Yankees, under the leadership of the sainted Joe Torre, are on their way to a World Series sweep. And the year is 1998—oops!—make that 1999. Yet even though baseball's year was dominated by the usual suspects, no one was complaining.

Once again, McGwire applied a last-minute surge to trump Sosa in the home-run count, finishing with 65 to Sammy's 63. Meanwhile, Big Mac erased the one blemish on his halo, giving up the muscle-builder androstenedione, averring he wished to set a good example for kids.

Season's end found fans in four cities saying farewell to their ball parks. The folks in Houston, Seattle and San Francisco might not miss the Astrodome, Kingdome and Candlestick Park. But with the closing of Detroit's Tiger Stadium, built in 1912, the game lost one of its most hallowed grounds. Postseason play brought a pair of exciting league-championship series. The Atlanta Braves survived an exhausting, rain-sodden rumble against the scrappy, surprising New York Mets for the National League championship—an epic six-game brawl that was decided by a total of seven runs. The last pair of games comprised 26 innings of struggle more nearly reminiscent of a rugby match than of sunlit summer afternoons at the ball park.

In the American League, the Boston Red Sox's lightning comeback against the Cleveland Indians in the first round was more histrionic than their testy five-game loss to the hated Yankees, but not remotely as dramatic. No

Love 'em or hate 'em, those damn Yankees are too damn good—and the most venerable team in sports

script in baseball comes close to the 80 years of back story that informs all Yankee–Red Sox encounters.

The Series was a contest between the two best teams in baseball. The Braves were long on pitching, while the Yankee dugout was loaded with veterans who played best when the stakes were highest. Still reeling from their wrangle with the Mets, the Braves never seemed to show up, and the Yanks walked home with the sweep. The century ended with the most fabled dynasty in American sports racking up its 25th championship in 100 years—and when it comes to Series rings, a .250 average ain't bad. ■

When the Cheering Stopped

A quartet of champs leave the field of play—and leave no one to fill their shoes

CALL IT A GRAND SLAM—OR MAYBE A GRAND SLUMP. The single most dominant stars in four major sports, champions all, called it quits in 1999, and their retirement calls for a last hurrah. Wayne Gretzky is widely considered the greatest hockey player ever. Ditto basketball's Michael Jordan and Steffi Graf in women's tennis. And John Elway? Well, Coach, which quarterback would you pick to lead your team to a last-second rally? ■

WAYNE GRETZKY Age: 38. Seasons: 20. 61 records, including 894 goals, 1,963 assists

JOHN ELWAY Age: 38. Seasons: 16. Five Super Bowls, two titles. Records: total victories, 148; last-minute game-winning drives, 47

STEFFI GRAF Age: 30. Seasons: 17. Six Wimbledon and French Open titles, four U.S. and Australian Open titles. Grand Slam, 1988

MICHAEL JORDAN Age: 35. Seasons: 11. Six NBA titles, five-time MVP. 29,277 points

People

The Ride of His Life

The three-week, 2,287-mile Tour de France, Europe's premier bicycle race, is one of the world's great tests of human endurance. Every summer more than 10 million fans line the roadsides to watch the riders sprint, climb and sweat their way through every variety of French landscape. The Tour finishes on the Champs-Elysées in Paris, where the winner gets a hero's welcome.

ARMSTRONG: The comeback kid

In a sense, Lance Armstrong started the race a hero. In 1996 the Texas-born cyclist was found to be suffering from cancer that had spread to his brain and lungs. The prognosis could not have been grimmer. But he came back—and at the end of 1999's grueling event, the 27-year-old Armstrong was crowned the winner.

After the cancer was diagnosed, Armstrong says, "The first thing I thought was, 'Oh, no! My career's in jeopardy!' Then they kept finding new problems, and I forgot about my career—I was more worried about making it to my next birthday." Make it he did, after three months of debilitating chemotherapy and a brain operation to remove the tumors. Said he: "I'm a better person . . . a happier person than I was before." As were his millions of admirers.

Now, B-ball's Duncan Era?

Pro basketball's 1998-99 season was a passel of oddities. The first 32 games on the schedule were canceled because of a labor dispute, and at the end of the sawed-off year, the last two teams standing were the San Antonio Spurs and (surprise!) the New York Knicks.

It took only five games for the Spurs to beat the Knicks, who suffered from the absence of their injured big man, Patrick Ewing. The Spurs boasted a dominating duo: veteran David Robinson and the forward many hailed as the NBA's premier player in the post–Michael Jordan era, Tim Duncan.

In only in his second year as a pro, the 23-year-old Duncan was unstoppable. Tough on defense, strong under the boards and racking up an average of 21.7 points a game, the 7-ft. forward played with fierce urgency, yet maintained a calm façade that earned him the nickname "Spock." Live long, Tim—and your sport may prosper.

Racket Royalty

What am I doing here? Serena Williams, 17, asked herself in the middle of the U.S. Open championship tie breaker that would help her make history—and alter her relationship with her older sister. It was a moment of doubt. But she dismissed it quickly and concentrated on beating Martina Hingis.

Not to worry: Serena didn't lose tie breakers in 1999—not a single one. Including this one. Her triumph in the Open made her the first African American to win a tennis

DUNCAN: At 23, the game's best

Grand Slam singles title since Arthur Ashe won Wimbledon in 1975. And talk about sibling rivalry: Serena's older sister Venus, 19, had been expected to be the first in the family to win a Slam.

As for the men (remember them?), a new rivalry between Pete Sampras and Andre Agassi enlivened the courts. Agassi won the French Open, but Sampras beat him at Wimbledon. When Sampras

PAIR OF ACES: Serena and Andre dominated the Open

sat out the U.S. Open with an injury, Agassi rolled to his second Open crown. The new champ, single since splitting with Brooke Shields, celebrated by dating the newly retired queen of the women's game, Steffi Graf.

Images

LARA JO REGAN—GAMMA LIAISON FOR TIME

LIFE ON THE EDGE Look out below! That's Mark Lichtle on the left, BASE jumping off a 3,000-ft. cliff in Kjerag, Norway; a parachute will soften his fall. And what, you ask, is BASE jumping? Well, the acronym stands for building, antenna, span (bridge) and earth (cliffs) jumping. Though 46 jumpers have died in the sport's 18-year history, it is growing in popularity; there were some 1,000 U.S. jumpers in 1999, as more Americans embraced extreme sports.

The Titan of Tae-Bo

The Man of the Year? In the world of fitness it was no contest: the designation for 1999 went to Billy Blanks, the prophet of Tae-Bo, the year's most profitable exercise fad.

Tae-what? Well, think of it as the anti–Falun Gong: Tae-Bo is a grueling combination of karate-like punches, kicks and squats set to the rhythms of hip-hop. It is not for the faint of spirit or the weak of back.

Blanks, 44, was the fourth of 15 children born to a poor black family in Erie, Pa. "I was the one who wasn't going to be someone," says Blanks. He had bad hips, dyslexia and was nearly kicked out of his first martial-arts class at age 11. (Are you hearing the *Rocky* theme music yet?) Using a mirror to learn the moves and correct for his impairment, he remade himself. He won scores of karate titles, appeared in a string of B movies and was born again—in that order. Banks became a preacher in an athlete's body, and Tae-Bo was his one true gospel.

After opening his studio in California, Blanks taught such famed hardbodies as Paula Abdul and Wayne Gretzky. In August 1998 he brought Tae-Bo to the people—or at least to your TV—shelling out about $2 million weekly to air his 30-min. infomercial across the country.

By 1999 Blanks was a certified personality, turning up on NBC's *ER* and spending a week with Oprah in the Bahamas. And though some fitness experts faulted his tapes for inadequate warm-up time and instruction, millions of believers were happy. Tae-Bo videos may gross as much as $125 million in 1999—and they outsold the video of the blockbuster *Titanic* by 25 to 1. Now that's kicking butt.

SLICK KICKS: Billy Blanks leads a class at his gym in Sherman Oaks, CA.

Top to bottom, beginning with left-hand column: Stanislav Peska—AFP, Sion Touhig—
Corbis Sygma, Olivier Morin—AFP, ReutersTV, Mahfouz Abu Turk—Corbis Reuters Newmedia,
Mike Simmonds—EPA–AFP, Corbis AFP, Peter Petrov—Reuters, Lionel Cironneau—AP,
Mohamed Zatari—AP, Manoocher Deghati—AFP, Lionel Bonaventure—AFP

It's a bird, it's a plane—no, it's the last solar eclipse of the century, which cast a swath of gloom across Europe and into Asia in the summer, attracting a highly diverse group of observers. In a year when human eyes too often scanned the skies for approaching hurricanes or tornadoes, the cosmic blackout was a welcome diversion.

GOING ... GOING ... GONE! Pontiffs, Druids and Sikhs all became sun worshippers during the eclipse of Aug. 11.

Science

WAKE-UP CALL

Hurricane Floyd batters America's East Coast, leaving a trail of misery and destruction. Yet scientists say even bigger storms are on the way

FOR YEARS EXPERTS HAD BEEN ISSUING storm warnings, predicting the imminent arrival of Hurricane X, the killer weather event that the law of averages dictates must sooner or later bludgeon the East Coast of the U.S., making such legendary behemoths as Andrew, Camille and Hugo seem like mere squalls.

And right on target, in September 1999, here came Floyd. It was huge, spanning an astonishing 600 miles. It was intensely powerful, with sustained winds of nearly 155 m.p.h.—a Category 4 hurricane, only one step below the most destructive designation on the charts. Most significant of all, it was bearing down on the Atlantic coastline, putting millions of people and billions of dollars' worth of property directly in harm's way.

Fearing the worst, officials ordered some 3 million residents to leave the shoreline in Florida, Georgia and the Carolinas. The largest such evacuation in the nation's history, it created a media frenzy and massive traffic jams, including a backup on Florida's Interstate 10 that stretched 200 miles. Even Mickey Mouse ran for cover: Walt Disney World, near Orlando, failed to open for the first time in its history. At the Kennedy Space Center on Cape Canaveral, only a skeleton crew of volunteers was left behind to watch over launch pads and hangared space shuttles worth several million dollars.

THE SPIRAL MENACE: Hurricane Floyd hovers offshore, threatening Americans from Florida to Maine

WATER, WATER EVERYWHERE: And not a drop to douse a fire. So a Bound Brook, N.J., fire fighter can only sit—and fume

In the next century, we may face monster hurricanes whose 200-m.p.h. winds could

A last-minute northward jog by Floyd spared Florida a direct hit, and the hurricane mercifully hovered for long hours off the coast of North Carolina. The storm that finally came ashore at Cape Fear was far less powerful than the Floyd of just a day earlier. Even so, Floyd's rampage ran right up the nation's East Coast all the way to Massachusetts, dumping punishing rains from Florida to Maine and triggering widespread flooding. It left 44 dead; thousands more had to be rescued from roofs and trees where they had been stranded by rising waters. In hard-hit New Jersey, more than 650,000 homes lost power. Even New York City's famously combative Mayor Rudolph Giuliani quailed as the hurricane approached, shutting down public schools and appealing to workers to stay home as Floyd's rains battered the region.

But it was North Carolina that took the brunt of Floyd's damage. Floodwaters refused to recede for days, even weeks: some 30,000 homes were inundated and thousands more left without power. In the state's heavily agricultural eastern section, millions of hogs, turkeys and chickens were drowned. Officials put the price tag on Floyd's destruction at $6 billion.

For North Carolinians, Floyd was actually the second of a one-two punch of storms that will make 1999 a year to remember, if not fondly. In early September, Hurricane

Dennis pounded the barrier islands of the state's Outer Banks, then came ashore to unleash torrents of rain that flooded streets and caused extensive property damage.

Floyd's impact was much worse, yet it was nothing compared with the havoc that authorities had feared. Floyd came on like a lion but ended up as—well, not a lamb, exactly. Call it a sheep on steroids with a very bad attitude.

If it seems as though hurricanes are getting stronger these days, that's because they are. After a 30-year lull, the U.S. is once again being visited by hurricanes the size of the ones that battered the Eastern seaboard in the 1940s, '50s and '60s. Thanks to an unlucky confluence of events— warm Atlantic waters, brisk trade winds and long-term changes in global temperature—we're on the cusp of what could be an extended spell of very heavy weather.

Floyd is nothing, scientists warn, compared with what may lie ahead. In the next century, they say, we may see "supercanes" that far exceed Floyd's top sustained winds and approach a hurricane's upper limit of 180 m.p.h.— more than capable of sending a 30-ft. wall of water surging inland, flattening houses, inundating coastal cities and stirring the ocean bottom to a depth of 600 ft.

Moreover, that 180-m.p.h. speed limit pertains only to present conditions. M.I.T. atmospheric scientist Kerry Emanuel believes that over coming decades, global warming may breed still stronger storms. Atmospheric pollution and the greenhouse effect are expected to heat not just the air but also the surface of the oceans, and it is the thermal energy of that water that fuels typhoons and hurricanes. Emanuel estimates that sustained winds in future hurricanes could conceivably top 200 m.p.h.

WHAT MAKES HURRICANES? ESSENTIALLY, THEY are just big wind machines that move heat from the equator to the poles. While they do this very efficiently, the same task could be performed by swarms of individual thunderstorms. It takes a certain amount of magic, in other words, to set a hurricane in motion. First, you have to make the thunderstorms, and then "you have to get the thunderstorms dancing," as Florida State University climatologist James O'Brien puts it. "You have to get them dancing in a big circle dance."

In Floyd's case, the dance of destruction started when a disturbance high in the atmosphere moved off the coast of Africa and out over the Atlantic. Fueled by the rise of warm, humid air (in places, sea surface temperatures measured a steamy 86°F), the disturbance very quickly spawned a brood of thunderstorms that coalesced in a slow-moving whorl known as a tropical depression. On Sept. 8, as its winds reached 40 m.p.h., Floyd became a tropical storm. On Sept. 10, when its winds topped 74 m.p.h., it became a Category 1 hurricane. A few days later, as its winds approached 155 m.p.h., Floyd very nearly became a Category 5 storm, the highest rating of all—last seen in America as the 1969 monster named Camille.

CHRIS SEWARD—NEWS & OBSERVER

VICTIMS: Flooding from Floyd drowned hogs by the hundreds; here they're incinerated near Trenton, N.C.

send a 30-ft. wall of water surging inland to flatten homes and swamp coastal cities

The energy that made Floyd bigger than the average hurricane came from the warmth of the water below. The tropical North Atlantic in the fall of 1999 was unusually warm, as it was during the period of high hurricane activity from the 1940s to the 1960s. Then, between about 1979 and 1995, the tropical North Atlantic cooled, and hurricane activity slackened. Now, notes David Enfield, a researcher at the Atlantic Oceanographic and Meteorological Laboratory in Miami, temperatures in this sector of ocean appear to be trending up again. Like other oceanographers, Enfield believes this is the result of a natural climate shift, as opposed to human-induced global warming.

The increase in hurricane activity will threaten a coastline that has been experiencing a population explosion of remarkable proportions. Despite the dangers, despite rising insurance premiums, despite the fact that hurricanes roar through every few years, people continue to flock to the seaside. Moreover, the fat revenue stream from condo towers, resorts and convention hotels has made it very difficult to elect antigrowth politicians. More than 139 million people now live in hurricane-vulnerable coastal areas of the U.S., according to the National Oceanic and Atmospheric Administration. That number is expected to swell as aging baby boomers finish sending their kids to college and start looking to buy retirement homes.

As the frenzy sparked by Floyd demonstrated, it doesn't really matter where you live along the nation's hurricane belt: when it's time to evacuate, you're all stuck on the same stretch of highway. And that storm in your rearview mirror is closer than it appears. ■

AFP

CATCH A WAVE: A beach house is engulfed on Oak Island, N.C.

Around the World in

LIFT-OFF: And away they go, embarking from picture-perfect Château d'Oex, Switzerland

Capping a century of adventure, a pair of mid-air Magellans complete the first circuit of the earth by balloon

THE FIRST HOT-AIR BALLOON, THE MONTGOLFIER brothers' *Globe Aerostatique*, caused wonder when it lifted off from the town square in Annonay, southeastern France, on June 5, 1783, and drifted for less than two miles. Though balloon technology has moved on immeasurably from that first paper-backed fabric sphere, the sense of wonder remains. There is still something magical about the sight of a balloon rising slowly, cautiously into the air, searching for the current that will take it off into the blue. It lifts the spirits.

In March, spirits around the world soared when two balloonists came down to earth. Bertrand Piccard, 41, a Swiss psychiatrist, and Brian Jones, 51, a British balloon instructor, had completed the first nonstop circumnavigation of the globe in a balloon. Outdoing Phileas Fogg of Jules Verne's classic tale *Around the World in Eighty Days*, the two balloonists straddled the globe in only 20 days (though Fogg employed all manner of transport on his odyssey—steamers, railways, yachts, carriages, trading vessels, sledges and even elephants—the balloon was Hollywood's idea, not Verne's).

Fulfilling what sometimes seemed a quixotic fantasy, Piccard and Jones embarked from the Swiss Alps and brought their 180-ft.-high balloon, the *Breitling Orbiter 3*, down in the sands of Northern Africa. The stakes were different (a purse of $1 million, courtesy of Anheuser-Busch,

COSY? Gondola-mates Jones, left, and Piccard at ease

as opposed to £20,000 in Verne's tale), but their intent was the same as Fogg's. Piccard and Jones sought to prove a point—to themselves and the world.

When the *Orbiter 3* crossed the finish line (9.27° west longitude) over Mauritania, Piccard was ecstatic. "I am with the angels and just completely happy," he said over a satellite phone. Jones, for his part, said calmly, "I am going to have a cup of tea, like any good Englishman." They had sailed into history. And they decided to sail on a little more. "We do not land. We go to Egypt," Piccard radioed air-traffic control in Senegal. "We are a balloon flying around the world." Even their rivals rejoiced in the feat. "I will be

20 Days

Fabrice Coffrini—Keystone–AP

BREITLING ORBITER 3

Tent balloon
A small helium-filled balloon holds up a tent that insulates the top of the large helium cell

Tent

Helium valves

Helium cell
Provides the main lift for the balloon

External insulating layer

Appendix for venting excess helium

Propane burners
The altitude of the balloon is controlled by heating air, which rises into the balloon. At night the propane burners are turned on to maintain altitude

Fireproof layer

Cabin

Hot-air cone
Heats and expands the helium gas, increasing the balloon's lift

Tear-out skirt
In an emergency, the lower part of the skirt can be torn off, transforming the rest of the envelope into a gigantic parachute

Solar panels
Power for onboard equipment is supplied by five lead batteries that are recharged by a bank of solar panels suspended from the balloon

Oxygen and nitrogen tanks

Bunk

Toilet

Hatch

Kitchen

Control panel

Pressurized cabin
Keeps the two pilots comfortable in the extreme cold and thin air of the upper atmosphere. Carbon dioxide is removed from the air with lithium filters

Fuel tanks

TIME Diagram by Joe Lertola

tearing their eyes out when I see them," their erstwhile competitor Richard Branson, founder of Virgin Atlantic, told TIME. "But apart from that, I think a hug and a bottle of champagne will be appropriate."

The two succeeded where many had failed. Since 1981 there have been nearly 20 attempts to circumnavigate the globe in a balloon. Steve Fossett, a Chicago millionaire who attempted the feat five times, plunged into the Coral Sea after traveling 14,236 miles in August 1998. On Christmas Day, with partners Per Lindstrand of Sweden and Branson, he went down again off the coast of Hawaii.

It's tough for pioneers to make a name for themselves these days. Both poles have been reached, the Atlantic has been crossed and recrossed, and the eagle has landed. But Piccard had a legacy to uphold: his grandfather Auguste was the first to reach the stratosphere in a balloon, and his father Jacques dove to the deepest point of the ocean in a bathyscaphe.

Jones was the Mr. Fix-It of the expedition. He was quietly overseeing the construction of the gondola when he was nominated to be a reserve pilot in the *Breitling* attempt. But he found himself, as he puts it, "in the hot seat" when Piccard had a falling out with his first co-pilot, Tony Brown. The daring duo soon fell into a comfortable rhythm: Brian "made me a cup of tea while I was preparing his bed," said Piccard. In the craft's cramped gondola, solitude was not an option; the two ballonists shared the single bed in shifts.

As pioneering craft go, the *Breitling Orbiter 3* outclasses the Niña, the Pinta and the Santa Maria—and the *Spirit of St. Louis*, for that matter. It is a high-tech combination of hot air and gas, equipped not only with simple necessities like a bunk, toilet and desks but also a fax machine and satellite telephones. Its journey began March 1, Piccard's birthday, high in the snowcapped mountains

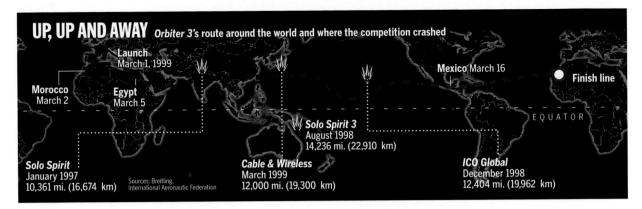

UP, UP AND AWAY *Orbiter 3's route around the world and where the competition crashed*

Launch
March 1, 1999

Mexico March 16

Finish line

Morocco
March 2

Egypt
March 5

EQUATOR

Solo Spirit 3
August 1998
14,236 mi. (22,910 km)

Solo Spirit
January 1997
10,361 mi. (16,674 km)

Sources: Breitling,
International Aeronautic Federation

Cable & Wireless
March 1999
12,000 mi. (19,300 km)

ICO Global
December 1998
12,404 mi. (19,962 km)

of Switzerland. Piccard and Jones cruised toward Italy at an altitude of 21,000 ft., crossed over the Mediterranean at night and enjoyed a meal of emu. On a satellite phone, Jones chatted with his wife at mission control at Geneva's Cointrin Airport, which was manned around the clock by a meteorologist and an air-traffic controller.

THE PILOTS HEADED TOWARD MOROCCO AND THEN turned northeast to catch a jet stream blowing toward India. In theory, balloons can't be steered, but pilots improvise by dropping up and down between different altitudes in search of the right wind pattern. Like surfers trying to catch a wave, balloonists try to ride jet streams, high-altitude currents that usually move from west to east. The *Orbiter 3* crew hit its target on the fourth day of the journey and sped along in a jet stream at 60 m.p.h. Once, when the balloon descended to 10,000 ft., Piccard ventured outside so he could chip away at ice that had formed on the cables and the capsule. The trip's only irritant was a mysterious buzzing in the cabin. On Day 5, Piccard located and dispatched its source: a stowaway mosquito.

On March 7 Piccard and Jones heard of a misfortune—and it was good news for their quest. On that day their competitors, the British team of Andy Elson and Colin Prescot, ditched over the Pacific. After setting an endurance record of 17 days, 18 hr., 25 min. aloft, the duo, in the *Cable & Wireless* balloon, was knocked out by a one-two punch. First, peeved that Branson's December flight had infringed upon its airspace, China denied entry to his countrymen, forcing them to follow a more convoluted route. Then, while traveling over Thailand, Elson and Prescot were hit by a thunderstorm that shredded their balloon's envelope. They survived, after a harrowing dunking in the Pacific.

Piccard and Jones had better luck with China. On March 10 the Beijing government allowed the Swiss-licensed *Orbiter 3* access to its skies, so long as the craft stayed south of the 26th parallel. Nevertheless, morale in the gondola started to flag soon after, as Piccard and Jones flew over the endless expanse of the Pacific Ocean. Progress toward Hawaii was slow, and they lost contact with mission control for four days. "I realized that the worst desert wasn't made of sand but of water," Piccard said when communications were back up.

Then the balloon popped out of its jet stream over Mexico and drifted in the wrong direction. Piccard and Jones were using up precious fuel without making much headway. Even worse, a heater faltered, and temperatures onboard plummeted to 46°F. Both pilots were exhausted, and Piccard had to resort to self-hypnosis to calm himself. But the duo pulled it together as their craft headed into the homestretch. Catching a 100-m.p.h. jet stream over the Atlantic all but ensured victory.

The names Piccard and Jones may not strike the same chord as Columbus or Magellan or Lindbergh or Armstrong. Indeed, the balloonists' feat is literally lighter than air. But Piccard and Jones have won the last world-spanning contest of our era. And now they are history. ∎

CORBIS SYGMA

TOUCHDOWN: After crossing the finish line in Mauritania, the pair sailed on to Egypt

WHERE TIME IS

Discoveries from high in the Andes and deep in the gorges of Africa yield new visions of our ancestors

BY MODERN STANDARDS, THE hostile summit of Mount Llullaillaco, in Argentina's Andes, is no place for kids. But the ancient Inca saw things differently, and so it was that one day some 500 years ago, three children ascended the frigid, treacherous upper slopes of the 22,000-ft. peak. They would not return. Once at the summit, the children—two girls and a boy, between eight and 15 years old—would be ritually sacrificed and entombed beneath 5 ft. of rocky rubble.

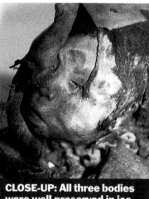

CLOSE-UP: All three bodies were well preserved in ice

And there the story might have ended but for the work of Johan Reinhard, an independent archaeologist funded by the National Geographic Society, who scales the Andes in search of sacrificial remains. He had already located 15 bodies, including the famed ice maiden he found in 1995. But these three, whose discovery he announced in April 1999, are by far the most impressive. They were frozen solid within hours of their burial. Two of the bodies are almost perfectly preserved; the third was evidently damaged by lightning. The children's internal organs are not only intact but still contain blood.

A wealth of artifacts was buried along with the bodies: 36 gold and silver statues, small woven bags, a ceramic vessel, leather sandals, a small llama figure and seashell necklaces. The head of one of the girls sports a plume of feathers and a golden mask.

Some of the bodies were provisioned with bundles of food wrapped in alpaca skin, which indicates that the children came from the Incan social élite. The preserved bodies will give scientists an unprecedented look at Incan physiology. Experts will analyze the children's stomachs to find out what they ate for their last meal, their organs for clues about their diet and their DNA to try to establish their relationship to other ethnic groups.

Later in April, an article in the journal *Science* announced three more exciting finds in paleontology. Members of an expedition working in Ethiopia uncovered a partial skull of a new species of human ancestor from 2.5 million years ago. They found fossilized arm, leg and foot bones—though possibly not from the same species—that may give experts important clues about how human ancestors were built in those days. And they also found evidence that someone was using tools to butcher animals in the same place at about the same time.

The new species was dubbed *Australopithecus garhi* (*garhi* means "surprise" in the Afar language). It was identified on the basis of a fragmentary skull with a complete upper jaw full of unusually large teeth that was excavated from Ethiopia's Middle Awash region. The combination of teeth and skull bones clearly came from a species more primitive than the earliest human, *Homo habilis*, who was making and using stone tools in the same region some 2 million years ago, yet more modern than known australopithecines like Lucy, the upright-walking protohuman who strode the continent some 1.2 million years earlier than that.

The evidence of butchery was even more exciting. The fossil jawbone of an antelope exhibits cut marks made by a sharp stone flake, which the scientists believe was probably used to remove the animal's tongue. A three-toed horse had been dismembered, the meat on its leg bone filleted. The leg bone of yet another animal is scarred by manmade cuts, chop marks and signs of hammering, presumably to get at the marrow inside. It was the earliest evidence linking tools with carnivority, an important milestone in human evolution and perhaps a factor in increasing brain size. The tool markings may not mean that these butchers were hunters. But it does suggest that they were able to plan far enough ahead to bring their tools on their travels. ∎

Mount Llullaillaco

Antofagasta

Area of detail

CHILE

ARGENTI

ANDES

60 mi.   60 km

Scale is accurate for east-west measurements only. North-south distances are foreshortened.
Mountains are vertically exaggerated.

FROZEN

SUMMIT MEETING: High atop
Llullaillaco, Reinhard readies
two bodies for further study

Images

SONIC BLOOM An American Navy FA/18 Hornet glides through the air over the Pacific Ocean, increasing speed in preparation for the moment captured in this remarkable photograph. Pressure created by sound waves from the jet as it approaches the speed of sound causes moisture rising from the ocean to condense into a ball of vapor around the nose of the plane. As the aircraft travels ever faster and finally breaks the sound barrier, the cloud is pierced and blossoms into a diaphanous disk.

Valley of the Lost Tombs

Move over, King Tut: you've got competition. Astounded scientists were comparing a treasure trove of Egyptian antiquities unearthed at a new, unsuspected burial site at the Bahariya Oasis, 230 miles southwest of Cairo, as equal in importance to the famous discovery of Tut's tomb in 1922. Unlike Tut's burial chamber, which had been partly looted, these tombs appear to have remained undisturbed since they were sealed some 2,000 years ago—more than 1,300 years after Tut, when Egypt was part of the Roman Empire.

The new site was discovered by Zahi Hawass, an eminent archaeologist who serves as Egypt's Under Secretary of State for the Giza Monuments. So far, Hawass's team has explored four tombs, with a total of 105 mummies laid on top of one another in neat stacks.

The remains were interred in four distinct ways. Some were covered with a thin layer of gold. Others lay under lifelike masks made of plaster-coated linen, or cartonnage, that was painted with scenes of ancient Egyptian gods and goddesses, including Isis, Osiris, Horus and Anubis. Still others were placed in so-called anthropoid coffins—pottery sarcophagi with human faces—

A gilded mask

and a few were only wrapped in linen. Bracelets, amulets, statues of mourning ladies, pottery vessels and figurines of Bes, whom Hawass describes as "the dwarf god of pleasure and fun," were interred with the bodies.

It isn't surprising, given their dating, that the mummies and their accoutrements have both Egyptian and Roman characteristics: the hairstyles on the anthropoid coffins are Roman, but the style of decoration is Egyptian. Hawass estimates that the cemetery covers several square miles and may contain up to 10,000 mummies. Once the huge, pristine site is fully explored, Hawass and his colleagues expect to have an unprecedented window into Egyptian life in a provincial town under Roman rule.

PHILLIPE PLAILLY-EURELIOS (2)

TODDLERS: These children were mummified like adults

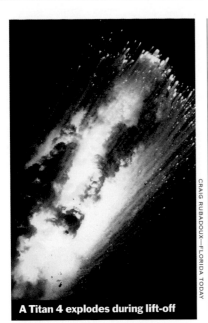

A Titan 4 explodes during lift-off

CRAIG RUBADOUX—FLORIDA TODAY

1999: The Year in Space

Rockets that exploded, cameras that failed, orbiters that burned up: a sometimes frustrating year reminded earthlings that the realm beyond our planet remains a perilous frontier. Among the problems:
• Over a nine-month period ending in May 1999, three Titan 4 rockets—direct offspring of a reliable 1960s workhorse, the Titan 2—flopped spectacularly. Each was carrying satellites worth hundreds of millions of dollars. One committed an explosive suicide 41 seconds after lift-off, the others misfired, stranding their satellites in useless orbits. Three other rockets—Lockheed's sleek new Athena 2 and a pair of boosters from Boeing's new Delta 3 class—also fizzled. Meanwhile two new rockets also failed in Japan.
• On Sept. 23 the unmanned $125 million Mars Climate Orbiter, designed to observe Martian weather, burned up as it entered the planet's atmosphere. Behind the snafu: engine-thrust specifications were not converted from English units of measurement into metric units.
• In August antinuclear activists assailed the flyby of NASA's large, complex Cassini probe. Defying critics who feared it might burn up in the atmosphere and spread radioactive plutonium from its generators, Cassini safely passed only 725 miles from Earth, hitching a slingshot-like "gravity assist" on its way to a date with Saturn in 2004.
• In December NASA lost all contact with its $165 million Mars Polar Lander during the landing process; the mission ended in failure.

Elated—Albeit Belated

Taking a giant step for womankind, Eileen Collins blasted off (after a couple of delays) on July 23 as the first female commander of a space-shuttle mission. Collins, 42 at lift-off, was a Syracuse University graduate, Air Force pilot and former teacher at the Air Force Academy with two shuttle missions as pilot under her belt. Within seven hours, Collins and her crew successfully deployed one of the most precious cargos ever to be taken into space: The $1.5 billion

NASA

COLLINS: Pioneer commander

Chandra X-Ray Observatory, a huge, sophisticated telescope that will enable scientists to study exotic phenomena such as exploding stars, quasars and black holes.

CLOSEST ENCOUNTER

On July 29, Deep Space 1 came within 9.3 miles (15 km) of the asteroid Braille

Deep Space 1's orbit

Asteroid's orbit

Deep Space 1

Sun

Earth

Mars

Asteroid Braille

Not to scale

Some 117 million miles from Earth, a small, unmanned ship named Deep Space 1 swooped to within 10 miles of newly named asteroid Braille in late July. The dramatic rendezvous marked by far the closest approach ever to an asteroid by a spacecraft and helped validate new and previously untried systems for unmanned spaceflight.

For 1,800 hours during its roundabout nine-month, 500-million-mile trek to reach Braille, the little craft was accelerated by a futuristic ion-propulsion engine that provided gentle but continuous thrust. And for much of its mission the ship operated somewhat independently of its controllers at the Jet Propulsion Laboratory. It diagnosed its own systems and navigated with the aid of an electronic brain reminiscent of HAL, the willful computer in the movie *2001: A Space Odyssey.* "What was science-fiction a year ago is now science fact," exulted Marc Rayman, the chief mission engineer.

But in this glitch-ridden year in rocketry and spaceflight . . . a glitch occurred. As DS1 sped past Braille, its camera failed to track the asteroid properly. As a result, DS1 produced only six tiny and disappointing images shot from 8,700 miles away, not 10 miles away. However, DS1's remote-sensing instruments downloaded streams of data that should reveal much about Braille's composition.

Since DS1 has consumed only 25 lbs. of its original 180 lbs. of xenon fuel, the spacecraft has enough oomph left to intercept and investigate two comets, one burnt out, the other highly active. If NASA gives the go-ahead, DS1 would reach those comets in—you guessed it—the year 2001.

The latest wrinkle in health is
eliminating wrinkles with a
laser beam. The latest wrinkle
in diets is eating all the meat
and saturated fats you like—
but avoiding carbohydrates like
bread and pasta. The pursuit
of better health is a gumbo
of science fact and science
fiction, of hearsay and
hunches, of this month's
fad diet or herbal cure-all.
It would be a fascinating
spectator sport—if it didn't
hit us right where we live.

OUT, DAMNED SPOT!
Cosmetic surgeons use pulsing
lasers to wipe away crow's
feet around a patient's eyes.

Health

EAT YOUR HEART OUT

Eggs are bad and margarine is good, right? Wrong. Here's the latest scoop on how you can munch your way to a healthier heart

A FEW DECADES AGO, TAKING CARE OF YOUR HEART didn't seem all that complicated to most Americans. You ate a balanced diet, didn't drink too much and got some fresh air and exercise—a round of golf, maybe. That was about it. Not that everyone, or even most people, actually lived up to these standards. But if you fell short of them, at least you knew exactly what you ought to feel guilty about.

Then we started hearing from the scientists. People who thought they were doing everything right, it turned out, were actually abusing their bodies—and in particular, their hearts. The cholesterol in steaks, cream, butter and especially those breakfast eggs was clogging arteries like sludge in a stopped-up drainpipe. Salt was poison: it drove up blood pressure and put an unhealthy strain on the ticker. Overeating and becoming overweight were a sure ticket to a coronary.

So, the thinking was, better cut out the steak, treat yourself to one egg a week, switch from butter to margarine and hide the saltshaker. Oh, and don't waste time with golf. Vigorous, pulse-pounding exercise was the only way to keep your weight within limits—and your heart properly toned. It was a spartan regimen, but it boasted the virtue of being comprehensible.

Recently, however, the scientists seem to have gone mad. Hardly a week goes by without some expert somewhere issuing a new report declaring that a particular food or vitamin or activity or condition will either restore your cardiovascular health or ruin it—and as often as not, the new advice seems to directly contradict the old. Among the recent findings:

- **EGGS** aren't nearly so bad for the heart as doctors used to think. Sure, they're packed with cholesterol. But scientists now know that eating cholesterol doesn't necessarily result in high levels of LDL, the so-called "bad" cholesterol in the blood, where the damage begins.
- **SATURATED FAT,** the kind found in red meat, butter and other animal products, may be a bigger threat to the heart and blood vessels than cholesterol.

- **OTHER FATS**—olive oil, other vegetable oils and the oil found in salmon and tuna—can actually drive down bad cholesterol and keep blood flowing freely.
- **MARGARINE** can be just as harmful as butter, if not worse; a process that stiffens vegetable oil into a butter-like stick also transforms it into an artery blocker. In general, the softer the margarine, the better. New butter substitutes, such as Benecol, can lower blood cholesterol.
- **SALT** has been considered taboo because it raises blood pressure. But it's not yet clear whether salt is a problem for those whose pressure is normal.
- **EXERCISE** need not be pulse pounding to be beneficial, say experts. A little gardening or strenuous housework isn't a bad prescription for cardiovascular health.
- **PHYTOCHEMICALS** are a whole new class of plant-based substances whose role in preventing heart disease may be even more important than vitamins. They fall into two classes: carotenoids, found mostly in orange-colored vegetables (beta carotene is the best known of them); and flavonoids—some 4,000 of them, found in, among other things, onions, broccoli, red wine and tea (green, black and oolong, but not herbal).
- **ALCOHOL** is good, in moderation. People who take an occasional nip of wine have about a 20% lower risk of heart disease than do teetotalers. The mechanism isn't entirely clear, but alcohol may boost blood levels of HDL, the "good" cholesterol that cleans plaque off arterial walls. Try two to four drinks a week for men, one to three for women.

New risk factors identified, old risks reassessed—yes, it all can become a bit confusing. So ... turn the page to find a chart that incorporates the best thinking of scientists and experts on how to eat your way to a healthier heart, circa 1999. ∎

PEANUT BUTTER

WHAT WE USED TO THINK
Has lots of protein, so it's good for you

WHAT DOCTORS SAY NOW
The kind sold in most supermarkets is full of trans-fatty acids, which are bad for the heart

WHAT TO DO
Eat "natural" peanut butter, the kind in which the oil rises to the top

OTHER NUTS
Nuts are a good-news, bad-news food. The bad news is that they're full of oils that aren't great for the heart; the good news is that they contain vitamin E

PEANUT BUTTER	♥ ♥ ♥
CASHEWS	♥ ♥
ALMONDS	♥ ♥
MACADAMIA NUTS	♥

SALMON OR SHRIMP?

WHAT WE USED TO THINK
Shrimp is relatively high in cholesterol, so salmon is healthier

WHAT DOCTORS SAY NOW
Cholesterol is a red herring. But salmon is high in omega-3 fatty acids, which may actually protect against heart disease

WHAT TO DO
Shrimp is O.K. for most people, but salmon is among the best nonvegetarian foods on the market

OTHER FISH
Salmon has omega-3 acids, and so do plenty of other fish. But not all sea and lake dwellers are equally blessed.

SALMON	♥ ♥ ♥ ♥	**SHRIMP**	♥ ♥
MACKEREL	♥ ♥ ♥	**TUNA**	♥ ♥
NORWEGIAN SARDINES	♥ ♥		
AMERICAN EEL	♥ ♥		
ATLANTIC HERRING	♥ ♥		
RAINBOW TROUT	♥ ♥		
LAKE WHITEFISH	♥		

MEAT VS. POULTRY

WHAT WE USED TO THINK
Red meat is higher in cholesterol than chicken, so stick with the birds

WHAT DOCTORS SAY NOW
Saturated fat is the real problem. Chicken is still better, especially if you

BUTTER OR MARGARINE?

WHAT WE USED TO THINK
Butter packs a heart attack in every teaspoon. Switch to margarine—fast!

WHAT DOCTORS SAY NOW
Turning vegetable oils into sticks of margarine transforms them into trans-fatty acids, increasing bad cholesterol

WHAT TO DO
Go for margarine in a tub or squeeze bottle. Or switch to a butter substitute, such as Benecol, that can boost good cholesterol

OTHER DAIRY
Butter is bad because it's made from saturated-fat-laden cream. But other milk-based products can also threaten the heart. Unless they're labeled low fat or nonfat, stay away from desserts and other foods that come from milk

BENECOL	♥ ♥ ♥
TUB MARGARINE	♥ ♥
BUTTER	♥
STICK MARGARINE	♥
SKIM MILK	♥ ♥ ♥ ♥
LOW-FAT MILK	♥ ♥ ♥
FROZEN YOGURT	♥ ♥
WHOLE MILK	♥
ICE CREAM	♥

avoid fatty skin and dark meat

WHAT TO DO
Order the chicken (but not fried)

OTHER MEATS
In general, the leaner the meat, the better—and wild game tends to be the leanest.

CHICKEN	♥ ♥
BEEF	♥
BUFFALO	♥ ♥ ♥ ♥
VENISON	♥ ♥ ♥ ♥
LEAN PORK CHOPS	♥ ♥ ♥
TURKEY	♥ ♥
LAMB	♥ ♥
VEAL	♥ ♥
HAM	♥
BACON	♥

OLIVE OIL

WHAT WE USED TO THINK
It's a form of fat, therefore fattening. Avoid it

WHAT DOCTORS SAY NOW
Your body needs some fat, and since it's mostly monounsaturated, olive oil is easy on cholesterol levels. In fact, it drives down the levels of bad cholesterol and triglycerides, both of which harden vital arteries

WHAT TO DO
Don't guzzle the stuff, but it's fine for cooking and drizzling on salads

OTHER OILS
Oils containing poly- or monounsaturated fat (like olive oil) are good; lots of saturated fat is bad

OLIVE OIL	♥ ♥ ♥
CORN OIL	♥ ♥
CANOLA OIL	♥ ♥ ♥
SUNFLOWER OIL	♥ ♥
PALM OIL	♥

Good News Marinade Aid

GRILLING MEAT OVER AN OPEN FIRE is a cherished rite of the American summer—but the process produces carcinogens. Now there's an appetizing alternative: researchers found that marinating beef for an hour or two before grilling can reduce the harmful carcinogens as much as 67%.

Bad News Bod-Mod

TATTOOING? TOO EASY. FOR THOSE who pursue the elusive pleasures to be gained from body modification (or "bod-mod"), the human form serves as a personal canvas to be cut, poked, burned and so on. The hottest trends in 1999: branding and tongue splitting. Catching the wave, New York City's American Museum of Natural History offered "Body Art," tracing 4,000 years of bod-mod.

Good News Friendly Folate

STUDYING VOLUNTEER NUNS OF THE School Sisters of Notre Dame, epidemiologist David Snowdon found a strong relationship between the severe brain atrophy of Alzheimer's disease and low levels of the common B vitamin known as folic acid, or folate. The message for you: eat more beans and salad!

Bad News Heads Up!

CONCUSSIONS FROM SPORTS ARE increasingly common, and two or more of them can impair mental performance. Some 63,000 occur every year among U.S. high school kids, mostly in football games. And as many as 50% of soccer players sustain concussions at some time.

Bad News Shingles Shock

HAD CHICKEN pox? Then get ready for shingles: 20% of those who have had chicken pox will succumb, for the virus lies dormant for decades before striking again, as shingles, often after age 50. The symptoms: skin lesions and nerve pain, frequently clustered on one side of the body.

Good News Bad News

We tried to balance the good news with the bad. But let's face it: it's the evil stuff (ticks! viruses! shingles!), not the good stuff, (soy?) that intrigues us

Good News Cold War

WELL, MAKE THAT "QUALIFIED good news." Gel Tech, the maker of Zicam, a nasal spray, says the stuff can insulate the nasal passages from a spreading cold, as Zicam's zinc ions retard the progress of the rhinoviruses that cause the discomfort. Scientists, at first optimistic, say more study is needed.

Good News The Joy of Soy

O.K., THE JOY OF SEX MAY BE MORE appealing, but researchers are finding that soy protein can lower cholesterol, fight cancer and build healthy bones. For the best results, stick as close to the original beans as your palate will allow: try edamame (boiled soybeans), tofu (bean curd) or a soy powder or concentrate.

Bad News Tick ... tick

HATE TICKS? HERE'S MORE FUEL for you: researchers have identified a new tick-borne bacterial disease called Ehrlichiosis, transmitted by the Lone Star tick in the southern half of the U.S. And it's hard to spot: there's no rash, as occurs in Lyme disease. Left untreated, severe cases can kill—so always check for ticks after hiking in the woods.

Good News SAMe Acclaim

IF DIETARY AIDS were films, SAMe would be a blockbuster. Introduced into the U.S. in March, the natural remedy quickly became popular as a treatment to fight depression and ease aching joints. The name is short for S-adenosylmethionine, a compound made in every cell in the body. Some say it's a wonder cure: it's not, but it does seem to be safe.

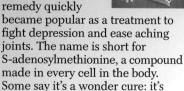

Bad News Aa—chooo!

SNEEZIN' SEASON: RESEARCHERS found that allergies affect nearly 40% of all Americans—that's twice as many as was thought. And millions of the afflicted suffer needlessly or rely on medications they'd rather not take. According to a 1999 survey, two-thirds of those beset with allergies are unaware of other treatment options, like shots, which are safe and effective.

CENTER: ESTHER HAKIM/ANDRE LAMBERTSON—SABA FOR TIME. CLOCKWISE FROM TOP LEFT: DIMAGGIO/KALISH—THE STOCK MARKET; JUDY GRIESEDIECK FOR TIME; OLIVER MECKES/GELDERBLOM—PHOTO RESEARCHERS; JAMES WORRELL FOR TIME; NO CREDIT; URBANO DELVALLE FOR TIME; ROBERT NOONAN—PHOTO RESEARCHERS; NO CREDIT; MIKE VALERI—FPG;

TIME Diagram by Joe Lertola

**Here's where high
blood pressure can
cause problems**

1 Heart: weakening of
the muscle; heart attack

2 Brain: stroke

3 Kidneys: organ failure

4 Lungs: organ damage

5 Eyes: blindness

6 Arms and legs: pain
and skin ulcers

Pressure Points

High blood pressure can be just as lethal as high cholesterol. It increases the risk of heart disease, kidney failure and stroke—and you've got it if your readings exceed the normal limit of 140/90 mm Hg at rest. Blood-pressure rates in America, once declining, are rising again—and so is the incidence of stroke. What to do: get your pressure checked regularly, and if you need treatment, find a drug that's right for you from the many available. If you're overweight, slim down. And here's no surprise: eating right (that means lots of fruits and vegetables) and getting plenty of exercise can decrease your need for medication.

Virus Bites Big Apple

At first the clues seemed random. Dead crows began turning up by the dozens at New York City's Bronx Zoo in July. Meanwhile two elderly patients with muscle weakness, fever and confusion were admitted to a hospital in Queens. The events presaged an alarming

LARRY WEST—BRUCE COLEMAN

encephalitis epidemic. By late November, lab tests revealed that the disease had stricken 59 people in the New York area and caused at least seven deaths in the region. Using trucks and choppers, the city loosed clouds of pesticide in the middle of the night, to the distress of many residents. Nearby towns quickly followed suit.

Then the culprit was identified: the mosquito-borne West Nile virus, usually found in Africa but also responsible for epidemics in the Middle East, Europe and Asia, though never before in the Americas. After the virus died down in the fall, experts identified it as similar to one that had been isolated in Israel in 1988—but they said learning how it came to America was more important than where it came from. The next question for scientists: Would migrating birds carry the virus south, to re-emerge in spring 2000?

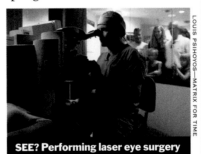

LOUIS PSIHOYOS—MATRIX FOR TIME

SEE? Performing laser eye surgery

Lasers In, Lenses Out

The hottest elective surgery in America is LASIK—short for laser-assisted in situ keratomileusis. In this procedure, an incredibly precise excimer laser reshapes your corneas—and you never need wear eyeglasses again. Nearly 500,000 Americans underwent the procedure in 1999, almost double the number in '98. In 7 out of 10 cases, LASIK corrected vision to a very normal 20/20. The cost: you're eyeballing around $5,000.

People

Low Carbs, High Profits

He's back! Dr. Robert Atkins, 69 in '99, was the poster boy for the year's hottest nutrition fad, the low-carb diet. The appealing weight-loss plans allow you to eat all the protein you want—steak, eggs, even fatty bacon—so long as you cut way down on carbohydrates like bread, pasta and soda. The fat-embracing diets, like so many other fads that we shouldn't have invited back, date from the '70s, when high-protein plans like the Scarsdale Diet and *Dr. Atkins' Diet Revolution* first made fondue hip.

In a single October week, low-carb-diet books clogged the top four spots in the New York *Times* paperback best-seller list of advice and how-to books. Bookstore shelves were jammed with volumes like *The Carbohydrate Addict's Diet* and a plateful of its spin-offs by Rachael and Richard Heller, *Protein Power* by Drs. Michael and Mary Eades, and Suzanne Somers' *Get Skinny on Fabulous Foods*. Atkins, a founding father of the eat-more-bacon movement, was back with *Dr. Atkins' New Diet Revolution*. Even bread-loving France had a best-selling high-protein diet book, *Eat Yourself Slim* by Michel Montignac, and Poland had the *Optimal Nourishment* plan. Russia would have had a book too, if it had meat.

Twenty-seven years after publishing his first trend-setting diet book, Atkins was sharpening his knives for a roast—and for critics like Dr. Dean Ornish, the widely respected researcher who has long advocated a low-fat diet for a healthy heart.

TED THAI FOR TIME

In an arts world increasingly driven by the live-or-die mentality of the marketplace, the best news came from the unexpected, the underdogs and the little guys—from pop music's new Latin beat to Hollywood's *Blair Witch Project* to publishing's spellbinding superstar, Harry Potter.

BOOK 'EM: British stage designers and directors Richard Jones and Anthony McDonald created this larger-than-life set for Verdi's opera *The Masked Ball* at the Bregenz Festival on Austria's Lake Constance.

The Arts

DREAMBOAT: Martin is an overnight sensation—after a lifetime in the business

Livin' la Vida Loca!

America, get ready to rumba! Led by sexy Ricky Martin, Latin pop is exploding

RIIIIIICKYYYYYYYYYYYY!" OUTSIDE A TOWER RECORDS store in Manhattan, a chorus of screams is going up. Mostly sopranos, a few altos, no tenors and certainly no basses. "Riiiiiickyyyyyyyyyyyy! I love you!" Some 5,000 people, mainly young women between the ages of *Dawson's Creek* and *Felicity* (with a few *Rugrats* and *Ally McBeals* mixed in), have gathered to catch a glimpse of the latest heartthrob, their *corazon*. The fans at the front of the line enter the store and stumble out with a signature scrawled across a CD or on a poster or even on their skin.

Some leave crying tears of joy. At a multiplex across the street, Fox is holding one of the first screenings of *The Phantom Menace*. You can see a flicker of hesitation on the faces of a few *Phantom* ticket holders. I thought I was in the red-hot center, the flicker seems to say. What's going on over there?

Ricky Martin was what's going on. The hip-shaking Latin pop star broke through with one of 1999's biggest hits, *Livin' la Vida Loca*. In early summer, his self-titled CD set sales records at stores across the U.S. And Martin was at the center of something bigger than himself. A host of other performers was bringing Latin sounds out of the barrio and onto the charts.

Ricky Martin was a fresh face, but not an entirely new one. For 15 years the 28-year-old singer had enjoyed a kind of second-tier, ESPN2 level of fame: he was a member of the teen group Menudo, he once co-starred in *Les Misérables* on Broadway, he had appeared on the ABC soap *General Hospital*. The wave he was riding—Latin pop—was not an entirely new phenomenon either. Salsa, rumba, mambo and other Latin musical forms have made inroads on American pop music for decades, with Celia Cruz, Ruben Blades, Gloria Estefan, Ritchie Valens, Los Lobos, Antonio Carlos Jobim, Tito Puente and many others scoring hits, exciting crowds and pioneering new sounds.

What was new is this: a new generation of Latin artists, nurtured by Spanish radio and

Tomorrow's stars want to look like Ricky Martin, sing like Marc Anthony and multitask like Jennifer Lopez

schooled in mainstream pop, was lifting its voice in English. Of this group, Martin was the hottest; Jennifer Lopez, 28, the most alluring; Marc Anthony, 31, the most artistic. With Hispanics poised to become America's largest minority group within the next few years, their music could be the sound of your future. Latin-tinged pop fits the musical times: it has a bit of the street edge of hip-hop, some of the bouncy joy of dance-pop and the fizzy-fresh feel of that ever sought-for commodity in pop, the Next Big Thing.

Puerto Rico is where it starts. An island inhabited by the descendants of black slaves and Spanish conquistadors, it is where cultures collided, rhythms intermingled, and salsa began. Anthony's parents hail from Puerto Rico, and Bronx-born Lopez also has roots there; Ricky Martin was born on the island.

Martin's performance of the soccer anthem *La Copa de la Vida* at the 1998 World Cup confirmed his superstar status internationally. He had done the impossible: he had sung about soccer in Spanish and got Americans to care. What could be harder?

SALSA RULES: In the wake of Ricky Martin's crossover success, Americans are embracing a new crop of talented, camera-friendly Latin singers. From top, Jennifer Lopez, Enrique Iglesias, Shakira and Marc Anthony

A French-language ode to cricket? His sexy performance at February's Grammys was another smash: the gloomy Beck stood and clapped, Madonna signed on for a duet. Martin's Stateside career was launched.

Lopez's career was skyrocketing along with Martin's. The experience of playing murdered Tejano star Selena in a 1997 biopic inspired the actress to launch a singing career. Her album, *On the 6*, sold 3 million copies. Lopez's talent lies in its diversity—she sings, she can act, and, as a former *In Living Color* "Fly Girl," she can dance.

Marc Anthony, the singer's first album in English, was another hit—not high art, perhaps, but the kind of relentlessly affable confection that transcends radio formats, crosses generations and sells like crazy. 1999 was a career year for the young star: he had a featured role in Martin Scorsese's film *Bringing Out the Dead* and teamed up with Lopez on *No Me Ames*, a hit on Spanish-language radio.

Hot on the heels of Latin pop's big three was a wave of wannabes, including heartthrob Enrique Iglesias (yes, Julio's son) and Colombian-born Shakira. And don't forget the old wave: in one of the year's biggest musical surprises, '60s star Carlos Santana enjoyed a monster hit with his album *Supernatural*.

Trends come and go, stars wink and fade out. How long will this new crop hold out? "[Martin, Anthony and Lopez] could have a longer career than most," says Wayne Isaak, executive vice president of music and talent for VH1. "Even if their pop following wanes a bit, they will always have this Latin fan base that can keep them playing Madison Square Garden and working with the best producers of the day." In other words—here comes the chorus—livin' *la vida loca*. ∎

Author J.K. Rowling has an uncanny ability to nourish the human hunger for good old-fashioned enchantment

Wild About Harry

Hero of a series of magical best sellers, Harry Potter isn't just for kids. Here's why adults have fallen under his spell

THE PUBLISHING PHENOMENON OF 1999 WAS A YOUNG British schoolboy with the unassuming name of Harry Potter. And if you don't know who he is by now—well, simply place yourself in the vicinity of a child and say the magic words of his name. If, for instance, you utter this charm to Anna Hinkley, 9, a third-grader in Santa Monica, Calif., here is what you will learn: "What happens in the first book—Harry discovers that he's a wizard, and he's going to a school called Hogwarts School of Witchcraft and Wizardry. At the station he meets a boy named Ron, who's also going to Hogwarts ..." Given enough time, Anna will tell you the entire plot of a 309-page novel called *Harry Potter and the Sorcerer's Stone*, which she has read, she confides, "seven or eight times."

And that book is only the opening chapter in one of the most bizarre stories in the annals of publishing. In the be-

ginning, *Harry Potter and the Sorcerer's Stone*, or *Philosopher's Stone*, as the English edition is named, written by an unknown author named J. (for Joanne) K. Rowling, appeared in Britain in June 1997 as a juvenile-fiction title. Abracadabra! It careered to the top of the adult best-seller lists. The same eerie thing happened when the book was published in September 1998 in the U.S. Next came *Harry Potter and the Chamber of Secrets*, which proved itself, both in Britain and the U.S., as salesworthy as its predecessor. By the end of 1999, the first two Harry Potter books had been translated into 28 languages and more than 10 million copies were in print worldwide.

In August *Harry Potter and the Prisoner of Azkaban* finally went on sale in the U.S., to the delight of young boys—and booksellers—around the country. Many bookstores opened for business at 12 midnight; others offered customers tea and crumpets or steep initial discounts. Everybody loved Harry, though some conservative parents objected to the books' fascination with wizardry.

"It was such fun to write," Rowling says of the first Harry Potter book; she lives comfortably but not lavishly in Edinburgh with her daughter Jessie, 6. Rowling began writing stories when she was six. She also read widely, and calls Jane Austen "my favorite author, ever." She was writing a novel for adults when, during a 1990 train ride, "Harry Potter strolled into my head fully formed." For the next five years Rowling worked on Book One and plotted out a series of seven novels, one for each year Harry spends at Hogwarts. Though she is often described as a single mother who worked on the first Potter book in a café while living on the dole in an unheated flat, Rowling says the story is an exaggerated account of a temporary bad patch rather than a definitive portrait of her personal life.

But enough of his creator—what's next for Harry? Why, a Hollywood movie, of course. Its producers promise that lavish special effects are planned. Ironic, given that the Potter books contain no technology at all; at Hogwarts, light is provided by torches, heat by massive fireplaces. Who needs electricity when you can have a magic wand? ■

Sensations and Recriminations

The mayor vs. the museum: America's culture wars finally hit its culture capital

THE BROOKLYN MUSEUM OF ART'S EXHIBIT "SENSATION," a sprawling show of young British artists that opened up the latest front in America's culture wars, was a sheep in wolf's clothing. "Sensation" was an adman's dream of a drop-dead one-liner, a vanity showcase from the collection of British advertising mogul Charles Saatchi that generated more noise than it deserved.

Outraged by one work in the exhibition, Chris Ofili's black madonna festooned with elephant dung, New York City Mayor Rudolph Giuliani refused to pay the October installment of the city's $7 million subsidy to the museum. The city claimed that the museum, in league with Christie's auction house, a sponsor of the show and the seller of $2.6 million of Saatchi's art in 1988, was knowingly trying to raise the value of Saatchi's collection. The city then filed suit to throw the museum—one of the country's finest—out of the gracious city-owned building that has been its home for more than 100 years.

Propelled by the whiff of scandal, "Sensation" gained greater attention than any marketing campaign could have garnered. The bad news: while some works had distinctive jolts of visual energy, corrosive or not, the exhibit traded shock for shallowness with all the easy insouciance of youth. That was surely the case with its lightning rod, Ofili's *The Holy Virgin Mary* (1996). The drawing of an African Mary (Ofili is of Nigerian descent) is plausible, but there is no real depth, no great feeling in the line. Ofili racks up the voltage by adorning it with cutouts from porn mags of women's crotches and then adding to the rhythm of the work with clumps of elephant dung. It's a calculated come-on.

In work after work in "Sensation,"—some 92 pieces by 42 artists—the same calculation peeked its tongue-wagging little head out of the art. There was nothing to do but roll your eyes as you passed Sarah Lucas' *Au Naturel* (1994), a dingy mattress leaning against a wall with an erect cucumber shooting up from two oranges, with two ripe melons posed just alongside ... get it?

The show was obsessed with the body, leering humor about sex and yammering about death. Yet some works warranted respect: Rachel Whitehead's plaster and resin casts of the space around domestic objects—the airy volume of a room or the underside of a humble chair—are eerie, elegant and refined. And the alarming piece that first brought fame to Damien Hirst, the most energetic of the young Britons, still packed a wallop. *A Thousand Years* (1990), with its vitrine full of maggots and flies that swarm over the bloody head of a cow, is a little pocket of hell: nauseating, brutal, but its shock looks death terribly in the face. Not silly, not shallow, not shock for shock's sake.

Amid the outrage and grandstanding, some crucial issues swiftly showed themselves: Should the largesse of public funding be used to circumscribe free speech? Can unhindered expression, in its turn, become sheer offense? And how ironclad are the constitutional protections for edgy art that may amount to hate speech? Citing the First Amendment, Judge Nina Gershon of the U.S. District Court in Brooklyn ruled in early November that the City must restore the museum's funding and stop eviction proceedings. The losers: the mayor, who vowed to appeal the ruling, and the museum, which stained its image with a flimsy exhibit underwritten by questionable sponsors. The winner: Charles Saatchi. ■

A museum in Brooklyn, shock art from Britain, tactics by Barnum. Result: brouhaha

PHOTOS FOR TIME FROM THE SAATCHI COLLECTION

SENSATIONAL? Chris Ofili's *The Holy Virgin Mary,* above left, provoked the mayor's wrath; Sarah Lucas' *Au Naturel,* above, was all too obvious

Be Afraid, Hollywood

Boo! *The Blair Witch Project*, a low-budget, high-chills pop phenomenon, gives big-ticket studios the shakes

ARTISIAN; TED THAI (INSET)

SLEEPER: Directors Myrick and Sanchez encouraged Heather Donahue and the cast to ad lib lines and entire scenes

TWO DIRECTORS AND THREE YOUNG ACTORS WENT into the Maryland woods in October 1997 to make a cheapo horror movie. Twenty-two months later, their film was a smash ... and the talk not just of Hollywood but of America. The impact, sudden and seismic, of *The Blair Witch Project* was utterly unprecedented. Never before had an offbeat movie budgeted at a ludicrously low $35,000 so successfully stormed both the box office and the national pop consciousness.

By year's end, *Blair Witch* had raked in more than $140 million in worldwide box-office sales—and that's before the video, cable showings and other ancillary revenues. It is likely to have the highest percentage of profit in film history. Its success made indie-film heroes of its directors, Daniel Myrick and Eduardo Sanchez. And the marketers at Artisan Entertainment, who built fervid want-see for the film through cunning use of the Internet (their site scored 75 million hits in two weeks) have been credited with revolutionizing the way films are sold.

Faced with this minimalist horror film—whose clever screenplay makes it appear to be a self-filmed documentary of three filmmakers who get lost in the Maryland woods while tracking down a local witch legend—Hollywood both cheered and shuddered. Any movie that scares up business is considered good for the rest of the industry. But this one became a hit by breaking too many rules. No-star indie films usually make money with charm and sentiment; *Blair Witch* had neither. So the mass audience will accept something strident, elliptical, confrontational—what next?

The movie was shot with its actors' being put through an eight-day survival game. The three—"director" Heather Donahue, "cameraman" Joshua Leonard and "sound man" Michael Williams (the actors use their real names)—shot the film and made up the dialogue while directors Myrick and Sanchez lurked out of sight and played sneaky tricks on them. Don't let James Cameron hear about this!

In common with earlier indie horror classics like *Night of the Living Dead* and *The Texas Chain Saw Massacre, Blair Witch* makes a virtue of its seeming artlessness. The picture's dead air, ragged acting and extreme shifts of emotional tone throw the viewer off balance. This is not your standard Hollywood movie, whose technical finesse

It has no sex, no music of any kind, no demonic power tools, no shock cuts to the monster—no monster!

reassures even as it excites. It's unmediated, out of control, a blurred or garish snapshot of lunacy. There are no shock cuts to the monster. In fact, there's no visible monster! The audience sees only what the camera does. At night it is sometimes pitch black; for excruciating minutes, we are literally in the dark. The physical mayhem is limited to one conk on the head. Making the viewer collaborate actively in both the scenario and the scariness, *Blair Witch* tweaks Mies van der Rohe's dictum: here "Less is morbid." ■

On Broadway, the Salesmen Cometh

Two classic American dramas are revitalized in vigorous new incarnations

BROADWAY, LONG ON REVIVALS AND TERRIBLY SHORT on new plays, runs the risk of becoming a museum of the theater. But when the exhibits on display are as stirring as 1999's twofer of Arthur Miller's *Death of a Salesman* and Eugene O'Neill's *The Iceman Cometh*, and the stars are as splendid as Brian Dennehy and Kevin Spacey—well, which way to the Theater Museum?

Death of a Salesman has made perhaps a firmer dent in our consciousness than any other drama written for the American stage. The chief reason, of course, is Willy Loman, that all-American victim of his own skewed recipe for success. There have been big, bearish Willys, like Lee J. Cobb and George C. Scott, and bantamweight Willys, like Dustin Hoffman. Dennehy, in the 1999 production from Chicago's Goodman Theatre, was a solid entrant in the big-Willy tradition, a charismatic man who, it's easy to imagine, might actually have been liked, even well liked, in his prime. Yet his lumbering frame seems constantly ready to tip over, a giant reduced to childlike confusion.

The famous eulogy that closes the play is perhaps its cruelest joke. Despite his brother's attempt to ennoble him, Willy's downfall is unrelievedly bleak. (Hardly anyone even shows up at his funeral.) That the play continues to fascinate us is testimony to Miller's ability to pack so much—heartbreaking family drama, an Ibsenian tragedy of illusions shattered, an indictment of American capitalism—into one beaten-down figure with a sample case. After 50 years Miller's play still makes the sale.

The Iceman Cometh runs nearly 4½ hours, has a garrulous first act that could try the patience of saints, and hammers home its central point about "pipe dreams"—the illusions that prevent people from facing the bleak realities of their lives—so many times that you might want to take a lead pipe to the author. Yet theatergoers deserve a chance to immerse themselves in this oceanic masterpiece. 1999's Broadway version was an inspired dip.

We're back in Harry Hope's bar, an end-of-the-line booze joint, where a dozen or so wasted regulars are waiting for the annual appearance of Hickey, a gregarious salesman who never fails to perk them up. But Hickey arrives with a teetotaler's resolve and a revivalist's mission—to get them to cast off their phony dreams. In this career-making role, which turned Jason Robards Jr. into a star, Spacey gave the performance of his life. Prowling the stage

Death of a Salesman is depressing, sometimes overwritten and painfully familiar. Yet it never fails to move us

in a half-crouch, his voice oozing with snake-oil and self-confidence, using silences as cagily as the torrent of words, he was funny, charismatic and ultimately shattering.

The Broadway production, directed by Howard Davies, actually improved a notch since its acclaimed 1998 run in London. Tim Pigott-Smith, as the disillusioned anarchist Larry, was an indispensable holdover, while Tony Danza as the bartender, Michael Emerson as a soused former law student and Robert Sean Leonard as a tormented turncoat were vivid additions. In their hands, a potentially grueling evening became a breathtaking experience. Sold! ∎

PICK ONE: Two great actors in two great roles: Brian Dennehy as Willy Loman (with Kevin Anderson and Ted Koch) and Kevin Spacey as Hickey (with Lisa Palfrey and Holly Aird). The Tony Award for Best Actor went to Dennehy

DAVID LEE—HBO

People

Funnyman of the Year

The funniest man in America? In 1999 the title belonged to Chris Rock. Dick Gregory called him a genius. Woody Allen said, "I'd love to work with him." As stand-up performer, and as the host of HBO's *The Chris Rock Show,* the 32-year-old product of a poor section of Brooklyn's Bedford-Stuyvesant neighborhood had the rare gift of making hard truths sound funny. It was an invaluable talent in a disinformation age in which it was more and more difficult to talk about things as they actually are. "Rock says everything you want to say but that you're not quite sharp or smart enough to think of yourself," said MTV president Judy McGrath. Rock on single moms: "It doesn't take a scientist to tell when you're gonna have f____-up kids. If a kid calls his grandmama Mommy and his mama Pam— he's going to jail." On white poverty: "There's nothing scarier than a broke white man. The broker they are, the madder they are. Poor, pissed-off white people are the biggest threat to the security of this country."

When Hollywood called, Rock refused to play it safe and make easy-money buddy movies; instead, he went to work for edgy comic directors. He had a co-starring role in *Dogma,* a film by Kevin Smith (*Chasing Amy*); a lead in *Nurse Betty,* a film by Neil LaBute (*In the Company of Men*); and a star turn in *I Was Made to Love Her,* for the Weitz brothers (*American Pie*).

Rock's work thrived on effrontery. "Somebody should always be offended," he said. "Somebody in your life should always be like, 'Why did you have to do that?' That's the difference between Scorsese and Disney."

The Perils of Pokémon

The Pokémon phenomenon wasn't exactly without precedent in the world of kiddie fads: witness the dashing Teenage Mutant Ninja Turtles and the dumb Power Rangers. What *was* new was the sheer relentlessness of Pokémon's multimedia and interactive barrage: it mesmerized kids into cataloging a menagerie of multiplicative monsters, with trading cards linked to games linked to television shows linked to toys linked to websites linked to candy linked back to your starting point—a pestilential Poké-Ponzi scheme. For kids, the key principle of Pokémon was acquisitiveness, and as card-trading began to make school playgrounds resemble Russian flea markets (complete with Mafia tactics), American parents were distressed. American conglomerates were not: they were cashing in on the action. Hasbro marketed the toys, the WB network swept up exclusive rights to the top-rated animated TV series, and Warner released the Pokémon movie, whose midweek opening spawned the "Pokémon flu," as thousands of kids called in sick from school. The man behind the curtain: comic-book and video-game aficionado Satoshi Tajiri, 34 in 1999, who first unleashed his "pocket monsters" as a Nintendo Game Boy program in 1996.

The Phantom Sensation

Talk about cruisin' for a bruisin': when it opened in May, *The Phantom Menace,* the first new installment in director George Lucas' *Star Wars* series since 1983, was the most avidly awaited, assiduously hyped film since *Gone With the Wind.* Burdened with expecta-

KEITH HAMSHERE—LUCASFILM LTD

TED THAI FOR TIME

JEDIS: McGregor and Neeson light up

tions that few films could satisfy, the new flick, with Ewan McGregor as a young Obi-Wan Kenobi and Liam Neeson as the Jedi master Qui-Gon, was panned by many critics and lots of viewers, but still reaped $429 million at the U.S. box office. Call it "richly disappointing."

1999 PIKACHU PROJECTS

POKEMON PLANET: The real stars are the "pocket monsters," not the humans

Images

ENCORE, ENCORE
Radio City Music Hall is perhaps the nation's most famous showplace, and after a seven-month restoration that stripped it to its bones and then rebuilt it virtually from scratch, the grand **Art Deco** theater looked the way it did when it opened 67 years earlier. Decades of wear had faded the dazzling palettes in **Donald Deskey's** sleek temple of machine-age speed and sheen; at a cost of $70 million, hero restorer **Hugh Hardy** brought them back in all their splendor.

Queen of Hip-Hop Nation

The sound track of the '90s was the rhyming sound of rap and the rhythm-heavy beat of its backing music, hip-hop. Rap celebrated its 20th anniversary in 1999; the

HILL: Grammy was hot for hip-hop

first such song, *Rapper's Delight* by the Sugar Hill Gang, came out in 1979. Now the hip-hop style permeated the culture, pulsing from the films we watched (any Will Smith

movie) to the books we read (even Tom Wolfe rapped in *A Man in Full*) to the fashion we wore (Tommy Hilfiger, FUBU). In 1998, for the first time ever, rap outsold what previously was America's top-selling format, country music.

If hip-hop was king, its queen was Lauryn Hill, 24 in '99, founder of the mid-'90s hit trio the Fugees. Her solo album, *The Miseducation of Lauryn Hill*, sold a smashing 5 million copies, was nominated for 10 Grammy awards—and won five.

Final Answer?

Stash this fact firmly in your millennium time capsule: in the year 1999, the television breakthrough that rocked Americans was … the game show. Nobody expected fireworks when ABC unveiled its version of a British show, *Who Wants to Be a Millionaire?*, in August, with walking punch line Regis Philbin as host. But the first 13 episodes of the

show were an instant smash, accelerated by the unusual format of running on consecutive nights. Nor was it College Bowl. (Sample question: How many pennies in a dollar?). But it spawned catch phrases ("Final answer?") and imitators like Fox's *Greed*—and no doubt many more to come from Hollywood's knockoff factory.

THE BEST OF
1999
CRITICS' CHOICES

In the arts, the century ended not with a bang and certainly not with a whimper but with a buoyant *¡Olé!* It was a *muy bueno* year for Hispanic artists: witness Pedro Almodóvar's masterpiece, *All About My Mother,* and the music world's joyous invasion by Latin popsters. And it was a vintage year for animation: witness *Tarzan* and *Fantasia 2000, South Park* and *Toy Story 2.* New TV shows clicked (*The Sopranos*); old musicals still charmed (*Kiss Me, Kate*). There was magic in the air, as kids and parents alike thrilled to the story of a broomstick-riding British schoolboy. And there was the sweet joy of delayed gratification: Susan Lucci won an Emmy, after 19 years of hoping. *¡Brava!*

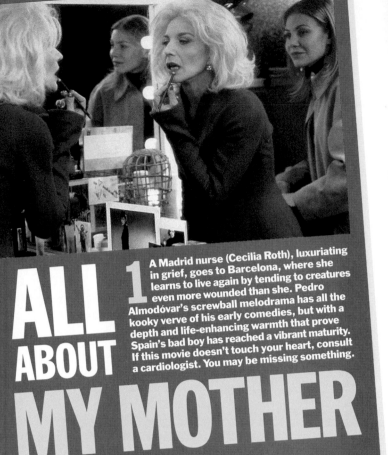

TERESA ISASI

ALL 1 ABOUT MY MOTHER

A Madrid nurse (Cecilia Roth), luxuriating in grief, goes to Barcelona, where she learns to live again by tending to creatures even more wounded than she. Pedro Almodóvar's screwball melodrama has all the kooky verve of his early comedies, but with a depth and life-enhancing warmth that prove Spain's bad boy has reached a vibrant maturity. If this movie doesn't touch your heart, consult a cardiologist. You may be missing something.

THE BEST CINEMA OF 1999

2 THE MATRIX With its dazzling effects and the dizzying ways it toys with reality, virtual and actual, this film may or may not portend cinema's future. But who cares about that when what we have from Larry and Andy Wachowski is a brisk, demonically hip, computer-driven reimagining of the dorked-out sci-fi tradition? A futurismo fashion statement and a can of whup-ass at the same time, it is smart filmmaking.

WARNER BROS. AND VILLAGE ROADSHOW FILM LTD.

3 TARZAN and **SOUTH PARK: BIGGER LONGER & UNCUT** It can be plausibly argued that there were more good cartoon features made in the U.S. in 1999 than there were live-action films. Disney alone had *Tarzan* (its snazziest and most affecting feature since *The Lion King*), *Fantasia 2000* (seven new sequences and an old favorite, *The Sorcerer's Apprentice*, in a rhapsody of sound and light) and, via Pixar, the deft, ingratiating *Toy Story 2*, which simply devoured the Thanksgiving box office.

And what can we say about Trey Parker's very un-

Disney *South Park* that the film itself didn't sing in four-letter words and the cleverest original movie score in decades? Just that the film is devilishly, hummably funny—if you can tolerate a heavy dose of inspired comic rudeness.

4 THE END OF THE AFFAIR This may be Graham Greene's best novel; surely Neil Jordan's starkly disciplined film is the best screen adaptation of any of Greene's fictions. An account of a slightly slutty woman's unlikely transformation into something like sainthood, it is acted with stunning austerity by Julianne Moore and Ralph Fiennes.

5 ROSETTA She is the teenager who will do *anything* to get any job, however menial. Luc and Jean-Pierre Dardenne's dour Belgian drama was awarded the top prize at Cannes in '99 by being both grinding in its sheer bleakness and inspiring in its intensity. Emilie Dequenne plays the title character with a blank, uninflected fury that suggests a medieval saint or a modern assassin.

6 AMERICAN BEAUTY Yes, some of the shots at suburbia are cheap (though it's tough to resist a movie whose villains are Realtors). Yes, Kevin Spacey undergoes an all too familiar mid-life crisis. But Sam Mendes directs with vivifying fresh-

ness, and Spacey's wicked performance as the cynical, bedeviled protagonist was, hands down, the year's best.

7 THE DREAM LIFE OF ANGELS If poor Rosetta had found a pal at one of her crummy jobs, the result

might have been this spare, coiled first feature from France's Erick Zonca. Marie (Natacha Régnier) is broody, draped in doom; Isa (Elodie Bouchez) is a sunny vagabond. Their friendship and rivalry are beautifully observed, magnificently portrayed.

8 ELECTION Cold, driven, hilarious Reese Witherspoon cares far too much about a school election. Matthew Broderick, the teacher supervising it, goes into sexual overdrive as he tries to cope with her machinations. And director Alexander Payne has made a dark, smart, sexy farce about the American ways of winning, losing and screwing up.

9 THE TALENTED MR. RIPLEY Tom Ripley (Matt Damon) would rather "be a fake somebody than a

real nobody." So he pursues a fatal game of pretense in Anthony Minghella's devious twist on the Patricia Highsmith crime novel about patrician indolence and underclass yearning. In a handsome cast, no one can touch Jude Law for

golden gorgeousness with an undercoat of sadism.

10 THREE KINGS Calculated brutality and mindless consumerism exist side by uneasy side as American soldiers search for gold and find post-modern anarchy in the aftermath of the Gulf War. Writer-director David O. Russell's electrifying trip down the rabbit hole is bruising, amusing, scary, and yet finally very moving.

THE BEST **THEATER** OF 1999

THE ICEMAN COMETH

1 For all its faults, Eugene O'Neill's lumbering meditation on the human condition still puts to shame most of what passes for playwriting today. And Howard Davies' beautiful production from London brought it alive for a new generation. Kevin Spacey put fresh sparks into the role of Hickey, the salesman who sets out to rid the denizens of Harry Hope's bar of their illusions. But nearly every cast member contributed to an electrifying evening.

JOAN MARCUS (4)

2 CONTACT How to get the ailing Broadway musical off life support? Director Susan Stroman and writer John Weidman had an answer: Cut out the singing. Their exhilarating show is composed of three heartfelt love stories told in dance and dialogue accompanied mostly by a wildly diverse jukebox of pop records and enlivened by the performances of Deborah Yates and Karen Ziemba.

3 THE LONESOME WEST Martin McDonagh continued to astonish. His comedy drama about two brothers fighting over their father's money—the third of a trilogy that included last season's *The Beauty Queen of Leenane*—played at first like a Two Stooges farce. But the laughs thinly disguised a chilling picture of human nature at its nastiest and a rebuke to the mythic romance of rural Ireland.

4 ANNIE GET YOUR GUN and **KISS ME, KATE** O.K., it's sad that the best musicals on Broadway are so often the old ones, but when you leave the theater on such a high, it's hard to complain. Bernadette Peters freed

Irving Berlin's Annie Oakley from the iron grip of Ethel Merman in Graciela Daniele's revisionist production. Michael Blakemore played it straighter with *Kate* but gave stars Brian Stokes Mitchell and Marin Mazzie a terrific showcase.

5 SPINNING INTO BUTTER A small Vermont college is the setting for this edgy exploration of racism and political correctness, touched off by some anonymous hate letters. Rebecca Gilman's searching play, at Chicago's Goodman Theatre, showed a keen eye for the culture of academic life but successfully resisted the urge to lecture.

6 ARTHUR MILLER At 84, he was hot again. First came a new production of *Death of a Salesman*, with Brian Dennehy putting his huge, bearlike grip on Willy Loman, then a powerful new opera based on *A View from the Bridge* and an impressive Broadway revival of *The Price*, Miller's underrated 1968 drama about two brothers coming to terms after their father's death.

7 BASH Three monologues by Neil LaBute, each exposing the dark deeds hidden behind ordinary faces. His pessimism is a bit forced, but LaBute writes sharp dialogue and creates juicy roles, two of which gave Calista Flockhart a chance to help us forget *Ally McBeal*.

8 CLOSER Patrick Marber's bruising drama about relationships is at its weakest when it tries most to shock, as in its central cybersex scene. But as a portrait of the way modern urbanites strive and fail to connect, it makes an impact. The Broadway cast of this British import, headed by the fine Natasha Richardson, could hardly have been bettered.

9 SNAKEBIT A fine actor, David Marshall Grant (*Angels in America*), has evolved into an even better playwright. With passion and sharp humor, his off-Broadway drama, about a trio of smart and smart-alecky friends trying to shift the course of their lives, digs deep into the souls of characters whose problems are all too universal.

10 JITNEY With all the fashionable cynicism around, August Wilson's warm-spirited embrace of his characters looks almost radical. This early work, given a "definitive" rewrite by Wilson and staged anew in Boston and Baltimore, immerses us in the day-to-day life of a gypsy cab company in Pittsburgh, Pa., and proves once again that Wilson is one of our most accomplished dramatists.

2 FREAKS AND GEEKS (NBC) Television has rarely got adolescence as hilariously, soul-crushingly right as in this bittersweet paean to Midwestern childhood circa 1980. With a cast that actually looks and sounds like kids, not Gap models, *Freaks* takes teen-show stereotypes—nerd, burnout, clueless parent—and fleshes each out with humor and heart.

3 BARBARA WALTERS AND MONICA LEWINSKY (ABC) Walters' three-hankie national catharsis turned the impeachment marathon back into the good old-fashioned tabloid scandal it was meant to be. Ridiculed and infantilized in the media for months, Lewinsky was surprisingly sympathetic, confident, unrepentant and, well, telegenic.

4 STRANGE JUSTICE (SHOWTIME) Historical TV movies must be staid. They must tie up loose ends. Above all, they must take no artistic risks. Showtime's Anita Hill–Clarence Thomas

docudrama broke all those rules, telling the *Rashomon*-like tale that launched the he-said-she-said decade with arresting images and a stubborn refusal to take sides.

5 CNBC DAYTIME Like CNN and the Gulf War or Court TV and O.J., the financial-news net defined the boom era with its sharp, zesty, sports-jock-style coverage. In 1999, the business of America was business news; CNBC's ticker—seen in bars, gyms, airports—was the frantic EKG of a stock-crazed, mercantile land.

6 MONSTER.COM'S WHEN I GROW UP A good Sunday-football ad is about dread—over money (investments), mortality (insurance) and, here, going back to work on Monday morning. In the job site's Super Bowl spot, straight-faced kids recited career "dreams" ("I want to be forced into early retirement") that spoofed not only the rat race but other ads' phony, chicken-soup-for-the-sell affirmations.

7 AN AMERICAN LOVE STORY (PBS) Ten hours inside the lives of an interracial family, this affecting documentary showed the import and irrelevance, arbitrariness and inescapability of race. With TV "diversity" limited to *Friends* for some Americans, *Moesha* for others, this picture of real integration was overdue.

8 SEX AND THE CITY (HBO) Carrie Bradshaw (Sarah Jessica Parker) and friends patrol Manhattan like a Fantastic Four whose weapons include sarcasm and Prada. Maturing in 1999 from a raunchy romp into an arch cultural dispatch, it's a refreshing story of professional women who don't need the love of a good man so much as want it.

9 BUFFY THE VAMPIRE SLAYER: SEASON FINALE (WB) Like the Littleton shootings—which prompted its postponement, one of TV's several craven post-Columbine p.r. gestures—Buffy's wry, touching season ender exposed the demons that lurk in even the most prosperous suburbs. Werewolf Oz's words after the episode's climactic battle scene—"We survived … high school"—were a resonant caption to the year of the troubled teen.

10 THE WEST WING (NBC) Attention, networks: There is dramatic life outside precinct houses and hospital wards. Aaron Sorkin's White House series is a love story of people and their jobs that overcomes its speechifying tendencies and tics (half the action takes place as the characters stalk through the corridors of power) with verbal gunplay, public-policy triage and a welcome, appealing lack of cynicism—about, of all things, politics.

THE SOPRANOS

1 This HBO drama reinvented the Mafia genre with Tony Soprano (James Gandolfini, in front), a besieged, postpatriarchal, Prozac-popping capo not truly the master of his family or his Family. But the show didn't stop there. Structured less like an episodic series than a seamless suite, it redefined TV storytelling. Watch it weekly, and it's an addictive saga; watch several at a stretch, and its rich vocabulary of metaphors and motifs submerges and resurfaces with novelistic grace.

2 MORGAN by Jean Strouse. Regularly reviled as a ruthless predator, J.P. Morgan emerges in this well-researched biography as a shy and self-conscious titan who genuinely believed that his own financial interests were synonymous with his country's. A few times he was right. Morgan's road to wealth, it turns out, was paved with some surprisingly good intentions.

3 FASTER by James Gleick. Those who wonder why they never seem to have the leisure to sit back and smell the roses will find plenty of reasons in this lively, irreverent primer on contemporary life. Gleick examines how we became infected with "hurry sickness" and points out that such innovations as cell phones, microwave ovens and the Internet only exacerbate the symptoms. Once a task has been speeded up, going back is hard to do. Try dialing a phone number.

4 THE TRUST by Susan Tifft and Alex S. Jones. The Ochs-Sulzberger family has managed the New York *Times* for more than a century, generating both handsome profits and public trust. The meld is a tricky one, and this history looks at how it has been maintained and assesses the *Times's* transition toward the electronic brave new world.

5 THE BIG TEST by Nicholas Lemann. Each year, the Scholastic Assessment Test determines where hundreds of thousands of American kids will go to college. Lemann shows how this process developed and casts a gimlet eye on the concentration of so much power in so few hands. Is this any way to run a meritocracy?

FICTION

1 Readers have come to expect something more than gripping plots from Scott Turow's legal thrillers, and this latest offers a mesmerizing main character. Robbie Feaver, a successful lawyer who has been caught bribing judges in Kindle County, becomes a pawn in an elaborate federal scheme to trap his beneficiaries on the bench. Along the way, Turow's suspenseful story deepens into a meditation on the nature of personal loyalties and the shady space between ethics and the law.

PERSONAL INJURIES

MICHAEL O'NEILL—CORBIS OUTLINE

2 A DANGEROUS FRIEND by Ward Just. A well-meaning American sociologist arrives in Vietnam in the mid-1960s on a quasi-official mission to help prop up the civil government. What follows is a small, tense drama that foreshadows the wartime tragedies that lie ahead. Knowing how reality turned out makes this fiction not a whit less engrossing.

3 HARRY POTTER AND THE PRISONER OF AZKABAN by J.K. Rowling. The third installment of this phenomenally popular series takes its now teenage hero through another year of his education in the ways of wizardry. Once again, Harry faces a mortal threat, as he and his friends weather lively British boarding-school scrapes. Fun for all ages!

4 WAITING by Ha Jin. A doctor in the Chinese army wants to divorce his wife, who lives back in his native village, and marry a nurse. Years pass, and the doctor gets no closer to his heart's desire. The author's gently comic rendering of this ordeal won a 1999 National Book Award.

5 AHAB'S WIFE by Sena Jeter Naslund. While Melville's men chased whales in *Moby Dick*, what were the women up to? This novel's spirited heroine tells all and debunks the notion that 19th century American women were as "sweet and resigned" as Melville assumed.

NONFICTION

HOME TOWN

1 This fond but completely unsentimental portrait of Northampton, Mass., captures the joys and the sheer human cussedness on daily display there. Tracy Kidder lives nearby, and he spent years listening to his neighbors and walking their streets. His book is an extraordinary feat of reporting and writing, a vivid reminder of twinned problems: why so many of us flee the small towns of our birth and why so many of us miss the sense of belonging that such places inspire.

RAGE AGAINST THE MACHINE

1 *The Battle of Los Angeles* (Epic). Because Tom Morello—who can make his guitar sound like a harmonica, a pair of turntables or a street uprising—is the most thrilling guitarist in rock today. Because rapper-singer Zack de la Rocha mixes poetry and polemics into song lyrics that would do Chuck D or Bob Dylan proud. Because in a year in which a riot of rockers copped beats from hip-hop, no other band made the rap-rock union resonate with such ferocity and intelligence.

2 **THE ROOTS** *Things Fall Apart* (MCA). This Philadelphia-based band named its CD after a novel by Nigerian writer Chinua Achebe: very cool. While other rap acts rely on canned beats, the Roots play instruments (guitars, drums, etc.), giving their work unique vibrancy and depth. Let the cartoon gangstas cater to suburban stereotypes—the Roots are keeping it real.

3 **BRAD MEHLDAU** *Elegiac Cycle* (Warner Bros.). A 29-year-old pianist who displays not only promise but accomplishment. With classical grace and jazz improvisation, he has created a masterly album about loss; virtually every track has the liquid warmth of a freshly shed tear. Moments of genius in music are rare as diamonds. This CD sparkles like a display case at Tiffany.

4 **NINE INCH NAILS** *The Fragile* (Nothing/Interscope). Into the orgy of urgently escapist pop that ruled music this year, Trent Reznor dropped this monument to loneliness and psychic angst. A powerful and creepily beautiful rock-'n'-roll album, *The Fragile* brought hope to alienated youth everywhere.

5 **SANTANA** *Supernatural* (Arista). Let's face it: most '60s rockers have headed out to pasture. But

with a little help from his friends (Lauryn Hill, Everlast), 52-year-old Carlos Santana stayed alive by renewing the formula that once took him to the top: blues, Hendrix-style guitar work and chugging Afro-Latin rhythms. Rock history, written by lightning fingers.

6 **FIONA APPLE** *When the Pawn ...* (Clean Slate/Epic). Like shards from a shattered mirror, the 22-year-old singer-songwriter's latest album glitters with reflective surfaces and sharp edges. Apple's songs, richly produced and intimately sung, explore the opposite of romance: betrayal, breakup, failure to commit. Apple has matured into more than a pop prodigy, more than a girl, interrupted. As an artist, she is now a woman in full.

7 **KIM RICHEY** *Glimmer* (Mercury). "From the ashes some glimmer of the truth appears," sings this veteran Nashville thrush. But her wise, smoky voice doesn't languish in the ashes of self-pity or revenge. There's buoyancy and gravity, musical variety and sneaky lyric craft in this endlessly listenable set. Verdict: *Glimmer* glows.

8 **LES NUBIANS** *Princesses Nubiennes* (Omtown). Hèléne and

Célia Faussart, singing sisters from Bordeaux, France, boast a global sound: they take African rhythms and American soul and top it with a cool, seductive delivery that's universal, yet distinctively French.

9 **CONSTANT LAMBERT** *Tiresias/Pomona* (Hyperion). Constant Lambert's final ballet score was

roundly damned by critics at its 1951 premiere, then went unplayed for 40 years. This recording (performed by the English Northern Philharmonia, conducted by David Lloyd Jones and happily coupled with the ballet *Pomona*) gives a second chance to an authentic masterpiece.

10 **REGINA CARTER** *Rhythms of the Heart* (Verve). A breakout album by a veteran jazz violinist. Drawing smartly on the work of jazz fiddlers of the past—notably Stuff Smith and Stéphane Grappelli—Carter makes music that's wonderfully listenable and, at times, breathtakingly daring. The devil never played fiddle this well.

1 Best evidence that Tommy Lee is a leg man: He reconciled with Pamela Anderson after she had her breast implants removed

WINNERS & SINNERS

8 Best hope for British divorce lawyers: Prince Edward got married.

9 Most imaginative dating: Jessica Sklar began seeing now-fiancé Jerry Seinfeld only weeks after her honeymoon. Runner-up: John Clark, Lynn Redgrave's now exhusband, admitted that he fathered a child with a woman who afterward became his daughter-in-law.

2 Best reason to end the *Star Wars* series now: Jar Jar Binks.

3 Best reason to keep Garth Brooks singin' country: his stints as a San Diego Padre and as Chris Gaines.

4 Best evidence that Hollywood is more amused by itself than is the average Joe: cancellation of Jay Mohr's much lauded show-biz sitcom *Action*.

5 Best reason to log off: Carnie Wilson's online gastric-bypass surgery. Runner-up: nude pictures of Keith Richards posted online.

6 Best reason to resist beatnik nostalgia: actor Matthew McConaughey was arrested while playing the bongos naked.

7 Best way to kill ratings for the 2000 Daytime Emmys: give Susan Lucci 1999's Best Actress Award.

10 Worst news for *Playboy* centerfolds: Howard Stern separated from his wife and is free to date. Runner-up: Hugh Hefner is taking Viagra.

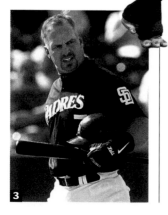

7

Nobel Prizes

Peace
Doctors Without Borders
(*Médicins Sans Frontières*),
for aiding disaster victims

Literature
Günter Grass, German
novelist. *"His excavation of
the past ... unearths the intertwined roots of good and evil"*

Chemistry
Ahmed Zewail, Egyptian-
born U.S. scientist, for
developing a way to photograph chemical reactions

Physics
Dutch theoretical physicists
Gerardus't Hooft and
Martinus Veltman, for
exploring two of the four
fundamental forces believed
to operate in the universe

Economics
Canadian Robert Mundell,
for his studies of the international flow of capital

Medicine
U.S. scientist Günter Blobel,
for research on the cell and
diseases such as cystic fibrosis

Tony Awards

Play
Side Men

Musical
Fosse

Actress, Play
Judi Dench, *Amy's View*

Actor, Play
Brian Dennehy
Death of A Salesman

Actress, Musical
Bernadette Peters
Annie Get Your Gun

Actor, Musical
Martin Short, *Little Me*

Sports Champions

Baseball
- *World Series*
  New York Yankees
- *College World Series*
  Miami Hurricanes

Basketball
- *NBA*
  San Antonio Spurs
- *NCAA Women*
  Purdue Boilermakers

- *NCAA Men*
  Connecticut Huskies

Football
- *Superbowl XXXIII*
  Denver Broncos

Hockey
- *Stanley Cup*
  Dallas Stars

Horse Racing
- *Kentucky Derby*
  Charismatic
- *Preakness Stakes*
  Charismatic
- *Belmont Stakes*
  Lemon Drop Kid
- *Breeders' Cup Juvenile*
  Anees
- *Breeders' Cup Classic*
  Cat Thief

Golf
- *Masters*
  Jose Maria Olazabal
- *LPGA*
  Juli Inkster
- *U.S. Open*
  Payne Stewart
- *U.S. Women's Open*
  Juli Inkster
- *British Open*
  Paul Lawrie
- *PGA*
  Tiger Woods

Tennis
- *Australian Open*
  Martina Hingis
  Yevgeny Kafelnikov
- *French Open*
  Steffi Graf
  Andre Agassi
- *Wimbledon*
  Lindsay Davenport
  Pete Sampras
- *U.S. Open*
  Serena Williams
  Andre Agassi

Hollywood Films

Domestic Box office
1. *Star Wars 1:
   The Phantom Menace*
2. *Austin Powers: The Spy
   Who Shagged Me*
3. *The Sixth Sense*
4. *The Matrix*
5. *Tarzan*
6. *Big Daddy*
7. *The Mummy*
8. *Runaway Bride*
9. *Toy Story 2*
10. *The Blair Witch Project*

THE OSCARS

Picture *Shakespeare in Love* **Director** Steven Spielberg *Saving Private Ryan* **Actress** Gwyneth Paltrow *Shakespeare in Love* **Actor** Roberto Benigni *Life Is Beautiful* **Supporting Actress** Judi Dench *Shakespeare in Love* **Supporting Actor** James Coburn *Affliction* **Foreign-language Film** *Life Is Beautiful*, Italy

Fiction

1. *Harry Potter and the
   Sorcerer's Stone*
   J.K. Rowling
2. *The Testament*
   John Grisham
3. *Harry Potter and the
   Chamber of Secrets*
   J.K. Rowling
4. *Tara Road*, Maeve Binchy
5. *Poisonwood Bible*
   Barbara Kingsolver
6. *The Girl Who Loved Tom
   Gordon*, Stephen King
7. *White Oleander,* Janet Finch
8. *Hannibal*, Thomas Harris
9. *The Assassins*
   Tim F. Lahaye
10. *Girls' Guide to Hunting
    and Fishing*, Melissa Bank

Non-fiction

1. *Tuesdays with Morrie*
   Mitch Albom
2. *The Greatest Generation*
   Tom Brokaw
3. *Art of Happiness*, the Dalai
   Lama and Howard C. Cutler

4. *The Century*
   Peter Jennings
   and Todd Brewster
5. *Yesterday I Cried*
   Iyanla Vanzant
6. *Conversations with God,
   Book I*, Neale Donald Walsch
7. *Bella Tuscany*
   Frances Mayes
8. *Blind Man's Bluff*
   Sherry Sontag and
   Christopher Drew
9. *The Lexus and the Olive
   Tree*, Thomas L. Friedman
10. *The Majors*
    John Feinstein

Top-Rated Television

1. *E.R.*
2. *Monday Night Football*
3. *Friends*
4. *Frasier*
5. *NFL Monday Showcase*
6. *Touched by an Angel*
7. *Stark Raving Mad*
8. *60 Minutes*
9. *Judging Amy*
10. *Everybody Loves Raymond*

SOURCES: BOOKS: SIMBA INFORMATION SERVICES; FILMS: BASELINE; TELEVISION: NIELSENMEDIA RESEARCH; ALL OTHERS: FACTS ON FILE

Robert L. Knudsen

"When we go back to the sea," said John F. Kennedy in 1962, "we are going back from whence we came." In 1999 the late President's son John and his wife Carolyn made that journey, were lost at sea and then buried at sea after their plane crashed off Martha's Vineyard. Others who left their mark on our times also passed away: a legend from baseball's past, a star of golf's present, the creator of *Dr. Strangelove* and a man who starred in it.

GOLDEN YEARS: JFK and son John enjoy an idle hour on a Rhode Island beach in 1963.

Milestones

John F. Kennedy Jr.: 1960-1999

A LIFE ONSTAGE: Growing up before our eyes, Kennedy became saluted his father's coffin; center, as a teenager with Jackie and

A Death in the Family

John Kennedy Jr. and his wife are lost at sea in a plane crash

JOHN KENNEDY JR. WAS SWADDLED IN headlines, the first baby ever born to a President-elect. It was news when he came out of the incubator, when he first went on formula, when he got a haircut or lost a tooth. His famous salute to his father's coffin came on his third birthday. The family never called him John-John; a reporter heard his father chasing after the fleeing toddler, shouting "John, John," and thought it was a pet name. And so it became America's name for him, not his family's, which was fitting: like the rest of the family, he was always partly a myth of our making, a mirror, a mirage.

If you believe his friends, the most famous son in the world wanted nothing more than to be a normal guy, to put people at ease. Born to a father who understood politics as performance art, he hoped at one time to become an actor, but wound up as an editor of a magazine, *George*, intended to treat politics as entertainment.

He lived life to the fullest, though in the shadow of the murders of his father and his uncle Bobby. He graduated from Brown, kayaked and parasailed and Rollerbladed through Central Park, dated Madonna and Daryl Hannah, flunked the bar exam twice, worked in the Manhattan District Attorney's office, and couldn't go for pizza without the tabloid photographers coming along.

Jacqueline Kennedy Onassis received much deserved praise for the way she raised her children. But John and his sister Caroline deserve credit as well for the character they displayed after growing up in America's battered, beloved, hated, almost-royal family.

In 1994 John's mother succumbed to cancer, robbing him of the single most important person in his life. He issued a note-perfect statement to the press, grieved deeply and permanently, but got through it. It helped that he soon fell in love with Carolyn Bessette, an exquisitely sophisticated Calvin Klein public relations executive. In 1996 they married on Cumberland Island, a windswept retreat off the Georgia coast, a home to wild horses. The chapel was a tiny wood-frame building lit only by candles and kerosene lamps. No members of the media were present; they had been skillfully kept away.

John's cousin Rory, youngest daughter of Robert Kennedy, was to be married at Hyannis Port on Saturday, July 17. The night before, John, Carolyn and her older sister Lauren Bessette set out to fly from an airport in Fairfield, N.J., to Hyannis Port, intending to drop Lauren off at Martha's Vineyard on the way. An avid but inexperienced pilot, John had earned his license only 15 months before.

The night was hazy, the visibility poor. The Kennedys were expected in Hyannis Port around 10 p.m.; when they had not turned up by 2 a.m., a family friend reported them missing, and a search was begun about an hour later.

Saturday morning the startling news spread around the country, and the vigil commenced. President Clinton was kept informed of the search's progress and began calling family members. But by noon it was clear that the plane had crashed at sea, and that there were no survivors.

Neighbors began leaving candles and flowers outside the Tribeca building where John and Carolyn lived. The crowd at Yankee Stadium, where John had spent Thursday evening, observed a moment of silence before the game. Churches held special Masses and prayer services, including one in Connecticut for members of the Bessette family, who were contemplating the loss of two of their three daughters.

The memorial service was held at the Church of St. Thomas More in New York City, a small neighborhood church that John and his sister had attended with their mother as children. "He had every gift but length of years," said Senator Ted Kennedy in his eulogy. The day before, the ashes of John and Carolyn had been borne out to sea aboard the U.S.S. *Briscoe* and committed to the waves not far from the beach at Hyannis Port, the beach where the young boy and his father the President had once built sand castles. ■

STAR POWER: John's good looks heightened his appeal

GREGORY HEISLER—CORBIS OUTLINE

TED MALLORY—NEWSMAKERS (TOP), UPI—CORBIS BETTMANN, STEVE LISS—GAMMA LIAISON, DAVID L. RYAN—THE BOSTON GLOBE

THE COUPLE: John and Carolyn radiated glamour but eschewed pretension

America's favorite son. Left, he Caroline; right, burial at sea

Joe DiMaggio: 1914-1999

THE SWING: DiMaggio showed off his long stride and classic follow-through in 1941

CORBIS BETTMANN

Left and Gone Away

Joltin' Joe was a myth—and more

DURING THE 13 SEASONS JOE DIMAGGIO PLAYED CENTER field for the New York Yankees, the 16 major league teams were clustered in only 10 cities. In that pre-television era, sports heroes were created out of words, those spoken on the radio during play-by-play broadcasts and those printed in newspapers the next day. No wonder legends arose. Most people experienced baseball by reading adventure stories in the daily press or by listening, like the ancient Greeks, to the voices of the bards.

GEORGE ZENO COLLECTION

DREAM DATE: Joe and Marilyn at the Stork Club in New York City, 1954. His love survived their divorce

Baseball's mythmaking machinery went into overdrive when the shy, 21-year-old Joe DiMaggio came up with the Yankees from spring training in 1936. Babe Ruth was gone: this handsome new kid, the son of a Sicilian immigrant fisherman, looked promising. His successful rookie season—top American League vote getter for the All-Star game, making the cover of TIME, winning the World Series—confirmed and enhanced the DiMaggio mystique. Meanwhile, the young man from Fisherman's Wharf was acquiring polish. He took up tailored suits, led the high life at Toots Shor's nightclub, dated beautiful women.

The defining event of DiMaggio's career occurred in 1941, when he got at least one base hit in 56 games in a row—a feat no other player has come close to matching. DiMaggio retired at the end of the 1951 season; he had been hobbled for several years by painful bone spurs in his right heel. Once out of baseball, he did the only thing that could further his mythical status: long divorced from his first wife Dorothy, he courted and in 1954 married Marilyn Monroe. Their union was passionate but star-crossed: he craved privacy and a quiet life; she attracted, always, a maelstrom of publicity. They divorced, but his quiet grief after her death in 1962 proved that the great poker-faced star had a heart after all, and the world could see that it had been broken. ∎

King Hussein: 1935-1999

ON DUTY: In 1970, midway through his long reign, the King watched troops on maneuvers

DOUGHTY KING HUSSEIN OF JORDAN WAS A SURVIVOR in the turbulent swirl of Middle East politics. He succeeded to the Hashemite throne in 1952, at 16; when he returned from an American hospital to die in his homeland after a long battle with non-Hodgkin's lymphoma in February, at 63, he was the Middle East's longest-serving leader. Ruling with personal courage and political caution, he navigated his country through the intrigues of the cold war to his goal of peace with Israel.

In the Middle East, the term survivor is no metaphor. Hussein weathered at least 18 murder attempts, coup plots, army insurrections and a civil war. His first two marriages ended in divorce; his third wife died in a helicopter crash. In 1978 he made an American his Queen: the former Lisa Halaby, the daughter of an airline executive of Arab descent, became the anchor of his personal life.

Though Hussein made costly mistakes—attacking Israel in the 1967 Six-Day War, supporting Iraq in the Gulf War—he emerged as the region's strongest force for moderation.

Hussein molded a modern, cohesive state from a collection of Bedouin tribes and Palestinian refugees, but his disappointments were legion: the loss of Hashemite rule in Iraq and the West Bank; the bittersweet peace with Israel; even the falling out with his younger brother Hassan in the last six months of his life. For many years he played a pivotal role in the quest for a comprehensive peace, culminating in October, 1998, when he gamely left his hospital bed to come to the Wye River conference and help break a deadlock in the U.S.-sponsored negotiations. For that perseverance in the name of peace—and for a lifetime of courage and tolerance in a part of the world so lacking in either—the world is in Hussein's debt. ∎

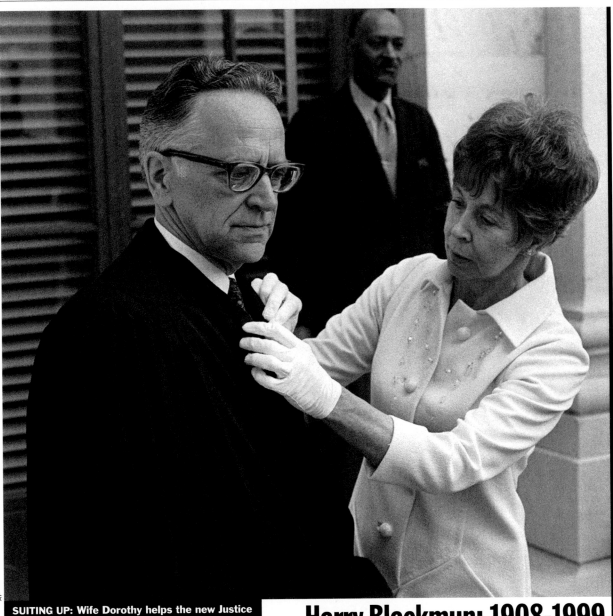

SUITING UP: Wife Dorothy helps the new Justice prepare for his first day on the Supreme Court

Harry Blackmun: 1908-1999

AMERICAN HISTORY HAS BEEN SHAPED BY A HANDFUL of Supreme Court cases: the Dred Scott case in 1857, which endorsed slaveholders' rights; *Plessy v. Ferguson*, 1896, which sanctioned segregation; *Brown v. Board of Education*, 1954, which overturned it. One of the most bitterly divisive of such rulings was *Roe v. Wade*, which legalized abortion. The Justice who wrote that 1973 majority opinion, Harry Blackmun, was named to the court in 1969 by Richard Nixon. When Justice Blackmun died of complications following hip surgery in March, TIME invited a fellow Minnesotan, radio host Garrison Keillor, to contribute a eulogy. His words:

"Harry Blackmun was a St. Paul boy from the East Side, the rough side, who got scholarshipped to Harvard, came back to Minnesota to practice law and landed on the Supreme Court at 61, an age when a man thinks about cut-

ting back. He was a conservative who defended civil liberties and championed the poor and oppressed and authored *Roe v. Wade*, which made abortion legal, for which he received reams of hate mail, much of which he read.

"He was a man possessed of integrity and kindness. Every day after lunch, Justice Blackmun took a walk to clear his head. He went out alone, in his navy blue cardigan frayed at the sleeves and his old blue overcoat, walked around the block and, coming back, stopped to listen to the picketers who gathered daily to protest abortion, some with signs that accused him of mass murder. He had respect and compassion for them. They never noticed him, the small lean bespectacled man with gray hair; his humility shielded him. Then he walked up the steps under the EQUAL JUSTICE UNDER LAW inscription, went in to his office and resumed reading the law, which was his work." ∎

CORBIS AFP

Stanley Kubrick: 1928-1999

DEEP FOCUS: A perfectionist, Kubrick pondered his last film, *Eyes Wide Shut,* for some 20 years

STANLEY KUBRICK WAS NOT, AS CARELESS JOURNALISTS insisted, reclusive. Elusive, perhaps, for his refusal of fame's odious obligations was a clarifying choice he had embraced, not a neurotic compulsion to which he had surrendered. This alleged anchorite was a constant presence in dozens of lives, in touch via phone, fax and Internet. He built his life and his work around a few simple verities: that our universe is ruled by chance, that life is too short, that movies ought to be primarily a visual medium.

Take the question of chance, and recall *The Killing* (1956), the first true Kubrick movie. The race-track heist, a model of rational planning, goes perfectly. And then the sappy lady and her yappy little dog appear—mischance personified—to ruin everything. Remember 1964's *Dr. Strangelove* as well. The strategists delicately poised the balance of terror, without considering the irrational likes of General Jack D. Ripper. Best of all, think of Barry Lyndon, heedless of mischance, which ever haunts him and which too soon brings him to his foolish end.

Kubrick was his opposite, haunted by life's brevity and the hopelessness of transcending the blighted human condition. Hence the desperate cosmic rebellion of Bowman in *2001: A Space Odyssey* (1968), leading to his rebirth as the starchild. Hence the doomed struggle to reform vicious Alex in 1971's *A Clockwork Orange*—our technology, our social arrangements will never be up to the task.

Kubrick's refuge was art, a fragile fortress against mortality. Many deemed 1999's *Eyes Wide Shut* a failure, but it bore the sense of danger Kubrick himself projected, the sense that he carried within his own nature the whole disordered cosmos from which he tried to wall himself off—wayward, willful, driven by wild, bestartling surmise. ∎

ATTENTION! Scott on the set, in costume—and clearly in the mood—for his Oscar-winning role

George C. Scott: 1927-1999

HOLLYWOOD LOVES A CLICHÉ, AND ONE OF ITS STAND- bys is the italicized incarnation suggested in a thousand movie posters: Arnold Schwarzenegger *is* the Terminator ... Sean Connery *is* 007. But when a stone-faced, hard-drinking, hard-living, nose-busted-in- a-fight actor assumed the title role in Francis Ford Coppo- la's 1971 war classic *Patton*, the cliché was conquered by the man: George C. Scott *was* General George Patton.

Fate brought the two together, for Scott was the fifth choice to play the World War II legend. Like most such classic meetings of actor and role—Rex Harrison and Hen- ry Higgins, Yul Brynner and the King of Siam—the conflu- ence was both a blessing and a curse to the performer. Scott was an actor of enormous range, a star who easily commanded the stage (four Tony nominations), the screen and television (three Emmys). Yet he may be remembered

only for his bristle and bluster, though he was capable of unusual subtlety in roles ranging from Shakespeare to Ben Jonson to Chekhov. Like Jackie Gleason, who played off a surprising physical grace against a fat-man persona, Scott—an imposing physical specimen—used a sudden lowering of the voice or studied hesitation to bring dy- namics and breadth to roles a less thoughtful actor of his size might have been tempted to overpower.

Scott set out to be a journalist, and he clung to the skepticism of that calling, refusing to curry favor in Holly- wood. Awarded the Oscar for *Patton*, he skipped the cere- mony, calling it a "meat parade." He claimed he acquired his celebrated drinking habits in the late 1940s, during a four-year stint as a young Marine digging graves and bury- ing bodies at Arlington National Cemetery. "I became an actor," he once said, "to escape my own personality." ∎

Wilt Chamberlain

Daisy Bates, 84, civil rights leader whose memoir, *The Long Shadow of Little Rock,* won a 1988 American Book Award. During rioting in 1957 over the integration of Central High, Bates advised the nine black students. With her husband, she founded the *Arkansas State Press*—a key voice for the movement.

Paul Bowles, 88, individualistic Broadway composer and author of *The Sheltering Sky.* Bowles delighted in rejecting American conventions. He lived as an expatriate—mostly in Tangier with his lesbian wife, writer Jane Bowles—and wrote disturbing tales of innocence corrupted by savagery.

John Chafee, 77, Republican Rhode Island Senator who promoted environmental issues and was a proponent of bipartisanship.

Wilt Chamberlain, 63, 7 ft. 1 in., "gentle giant" of the NBA and the only player to have scored 100 points in a game. An enduring star, his legendary rivalry with the Boston Celtics' Bill Russell enlivened the professional game.

Charles ("Pete") Conrad, 69, third man to walk on the moon. Conrad was one of the more colorful astronauts. Setting foot on the lunar surface he said, "Whoopee! That may have been one small [step] for Neil, but it's a long one for me!"

Quentin Crisp, 90, witty, flamboyantly effeminate author of *The Naked Civil Servant.* In his autobiography, famous for its lack of self-pity, the self-described "mother superior of homosexuality" chronicled youthful torment at the hands of homophobes.

Andre Dubus, 62, short-story craftsman. Dubus published his first novel in 1967. In 1986 he was struck by a car, leaving him in a wheelchair. He subsequently produced some of his finest stories, notably in the 1996 book *Dancing After Hours.*

John Ehrlichman, 73, pugnacious Nixon domestic-affairs adviser and leak plugger who was imprisoned and disbarred for his role in Watergate, which included planning the break-in at the office of the psychiatrist who treated Vietnam War critic Daniel Ellsberg. Ehrlichman often insisted the scandal was overblown.

Judith Exner, 65, rumored former mistress of John F. Kennedy and Mob boss Sam Giancana. A sometime Rat Pack associate, Exner claimed to have been a conduit between Kennedy and Giancana.

Clifton Fadiman, 95, impassioned essayist and critic dedicated to making intellectual works accessible to all. Fadiman judged Book-of-the-Month Club selections for 50 years; moderated the '30s and '40s radio show *Information Please;* and edited more than 20 anthologies.

James Farmer, 79, courageous, booming-voiced Gandhian who along with

Al Hirt

Martin Luther King Jr., Whitney Young and Roy Wilkins was one of the four great architects of the U.S. civil rights movement. Farmer's Congress of Racial Equality provided the nonviolent vanguard for the perilous sit-ins and Freedom Rides to integrate the public places and transport of the South in the 1950s and '60s.

Raisa Gorbachev, 67, wife of the former Soviet President who broke tradition by sharing the spotlight with her husband, emerging as a First Lady who had her own mind, her own style and, some said, her own American Express card.

Joseph Heller, 76, author of the darkly comic masterpiece of World War II aviators, *Catch-22.* Its title entered the language as a catchphrase for the irrationality of the bureaucratic mind-set. The former TIME promotion writer's other novels include *Something Happened* and *Good as Gold.*

Al Hirt, 76, corpulent pop and jazz trumpeter also known as "the Round Mound of Sound." During a five-decade career, he toured with Big Bands led by Benny Goodman and Tommy Dorsey, recorded more than 50 albums and won a Grammy. Ever affable, he was an institution in his hometown of New Orleans.

Horst, 93, photographer of the rich and fashionable. Born Horst P. Horst, he infused his dramatic, stylized shots of such glitterati as Marlene Dietrich, Coco Chanel and Andy Warhol with ashtrays and other everyday details, claiming that "my best pictures always have a little mess."

Hsing-Hsing, 28, giant panda. A gift from Mao Zedong to the National Zoo to commemorate Nixon's 1972 visit to China, Hsing-Hsing, whose name meant "shining star," charmed some 75 million visitors to the zoo.

Jim ("Catfish") Hunter, 53, Hall of Fame pitcher. During his 15-year career with the Oakland A's and the New York Yankees, Hunter won five World Series, pitched a perfect game, won a Cy Young Award and became the first multimillion-dollar player when he declared free agency in 1974.

Milt Jackson, 76, jazz vibraphonist and improviser who co-founded the Modern Jazz Quartet. Jackson got his start in Dizzy Gillespie's band and recorded with John Coltrane and Thelonious Monk.

Frank M. Johnson Jr., 80, uncompromising federal judge from Alabama whose rulings invigorated the civil rights movement. Johnson helped desegregate many of Montgomery's public facilities and cleared the way for Martin Luther King Jr.'s march from Selma to Montgomery in 1965. Governor George Wallace called him a "scalawagging … integrating liar."

Madeline Kahn

Madeline Kahn, 57, devilishly ditsy singer-comedian. A diva of light farce, Kahn was Oscar-nominated for best supporting floozy in *Paper Moon* (1973) and *Blazing Saddles* (1974). She won a 1993 Tony for Best Actress in *The Sisters Rosensweig*.

Tibor Kalman, 49, Budapest-born guru of progressive graphic design. Through his firm M&Co., Kalman promoted social activism and innovative, anti-Establishment design techniques.

DeForest Kelley, 79, actor best known for his role as the humane Dr. Leonard ("Bones") McCoy on *Star Trek's* U.S.S. *Enterprise*. On the cult hit TV series and in six film versions, Dr. McCoy battled Leonard Nimoy's hyperlogical Mr. Spock, whose

emotional pulselessness McCoy delighted in disdaining.

Alexander Liberman, 87, artist and iconic Condé Nast editorial director who set the style and tone for *Vogue* and *Vanity Fair*. His Expressionist paintings and sculptures appeared in the Whitney and Guggenheim museums.

Victor Mature, 86, handsome actor known primarily for his barrel chest. "Mr. Beautiful" starred in epics like *Samson and Delilah* and *The Robe*.

Paul Mellon, 91, cultural benefactor and environmentalist. The only son of famed financier Andrew Mellon, he spent nearly $1 billion establishing such treasures as the Yale Center for British Art and the Cape Hatteras National Seashore. For decades, he helped run Washington's National Gallery of Art, which he founded in partnership with his father.

Yehudi Menuhin, 82, icon of 20th century music and renowned humanitarian. A few years after stunning a San Francisco audience in his first major concert at age 7, the prodigy went on to play at Carnegie Hall, where colleagues had to tune his violin for him because his fingers were too small. New York–born, he lived in London; Menuhin loved the Beatles, jammed with Ravi Shankar and was consumed with using his music to promote world peace.

Akio Morita, 78, co-founder of Sony and the man most responsible for making "Made in Japan" a tribute. Scion of a 14-generation sake-brewing family, he gravitated to the world of technology, starting, in the rubble of postwar Japan, the company that he later named Sony. The company took off after it seized on an American invention, the transistor, and used it to power a portable radio. An ambassador who opened world markets for his country, Morita was also an astute marketer who proposed and oversaw the development of the ubiquitous Walkman portable sound system.

Iris Murdoch, 79, erudite and macabre British writer, philosopher and

DeForest Kelley

Booker Prize winner. In her 26 novels, including *Under the Net* and *A Severed Head,* Murdoch described in intricate detail intelligent and idiosyncratic middle-class characters in the throes of what she called "erotic mysteries and deep, dark struggles between good and evil."

Anthony Newley, 67, showman. He co-wrote, directed and starred in the 1962 hit musical *Stop the World— I Want to Get Off* and helped write the score for *Goldfinger* and *Willy Wonka & the Chocolate Factory.*

Joshua Nkomo, 82, father of Zimbabwe. Nkomo spent years fighting Britain and later white Rhodesia for independence. Despite Nkomo's leadership, his erstwhile ally Robert Mugabe became Prime Minister in 1980. A subsequent split led to bloody clashes that ended with a 1987 peace accord and Nkomo's

Yehudi Menuhin

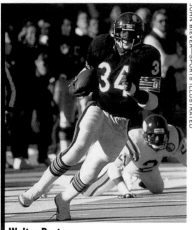

Walter Payton

appointment to a powerless vice-presidential post.

Red Norvo, 91, jazz's original mallet virtuoso (vibraphone, xylophone and marimba). Born Kenneth Norville, he changed his name after an emcee mispronounced it. A masterly improviser known for moody, delicate arrangements, Norvo led several experimental drummerless bands.

Julius Nyerere, 77, statesman and Tanzania's first President. Nyerere led his country to independence from British rule in 1961, united 120 ethnic groups into one country and was its leader for 23 years. He continued until his death to try to unite Africa.

David Ogilvy, 88, sharp-witted advertising progressive, promoter of long copy, the soft sell and co-founder of Madison Avenue giant Ogilvy & Mather. British-born and Gallup-

Gene Siskel

trained, he transformed such brand names as Hathaway, Rolls-Royce and Schweppes into legends.

Walter Payton, 45, Hall of Fame Chicago Bears running back who gained 16,726 rushing yds.—more than anyone else in NFL history. His kind disposition led to his nickname, "Sweetness," and his gallant stand against the liver ailment that killed him earned him enduring respect.

Jerry Quarry, 53, Hall of Fame boxer. Though he never won the heavyweight title, the popular pugilist put up decent fights against such ring greats as Floyd Patterson and Muhammad Ali. In later years he was incapacitated by dementia and a loss of motor skills resulting from repeated blows to the head during his three-decade career.

Jose Quintero, 74, Panamanian-born Tony Award–winning theater director and founder of Circle in the Square, a group credited with sparking the off-Broadway movement. Quintero directed more than a dozen of Eugene O'Neill's works, including the original Broadway production of *Long Day's Journey into Night* after O'Neill's death.

Oliver Reed, 61, hard-drinking British actor. Best known for his early roles in *Women in Love, Oliver!* and *The Three Musketeers,* he cultivated a bad-guy image offscreen, calling himself a "tawdry character who explodes now and again."

Harold Henry ("Pee Wee") Reese, 81, Hall of Fame shortstop and captain of the Brooklyn Dodgers in 1947, when Jackie Robinson joined the team and began the historic racial integration of the sport. The Southern-bred Reese's very public camaraderie with Robinson was crucial in dissipating the ugliness that greeted the rookie. Reese led the Dodgers to seven National League pennants and one world championship.

Gene Sarazen, 97, golfer and inventor of the sand wedge. Nicknamed "the Squire" for his diminutive size and

enormous panache, Sarazen won two major championships before turning 21. At the 1935 Masters, where he became the first player to win all four majors, he struck the "shot heard round the world," a 235-yarder, for a double eagle on the 15th hole. Four decades later, still sporting his trademark knickers, he punctuated his last tournament with a hole in one.

Glenn Seaborg, 86, former chairman of the Atomic Energy Commission and Nobel prizewinner. Seaborg began his career in the 1930s in Berkeley. He led the research team that discovered plutonium and was the first living person to have an element, seaborgium, named for him. After

Dusty Springfield

helping build the Bomb at the Manhattan Project, Seaborg championed the peaceful use of atomic energy.

Robert Shaw, 82, longtime music director of the Atlanta Symphony and dean of American choral conducting. In 1948 Shaw founded the popular, internationally traveled Robert Shaw Chorale. He especially loved working with amateur singers, whom he cultivated with a methodical, humorous style. "Singing, like sex, is far too important to leave to the professionals," he said.

Shel Silverstein, 66, children's author, playwright, *Playboy* cartoonist and Oscar-nominated songwriter. Silverstein was best known for writing and illustrating mischievous books of poetry for children (*Where the Sidewalk Ends, A Light in the Attic*)—a career he never intended, even though he sold 14 million books. He also wrote several hit pop songs and nine plays.

Gene Siskel, 53, movie critic who, with Roger Ebert, formed the incompatible but entertaining duo of reviewers whose "two thumbs-up" was one of the most coveted symbols of approval in Hollywood. More laid-back than Ebert, Siskel was no less combative. Their TV skirmishes, first aired on *Sneak Previews* on PBS, offered biting but sound-bite-size nuggets of ego and intellection.

Dusty Springfield, 59, British pop singer who first topped the charts with 1964's *I Only Want to Be with You* and hit her stride with her 1969 classic album *Dusty in Memphis,* which incuded the rowdy *Son of a Preacher Man.* She died just weeks before she was admitted into the Rock and Roll Hall of Fame.

Lili St. Cyr, 80, striptease artist. Born Willis Marie Van Schaack, she was famed in the '40s and '50s for her whispery voice and onstage bubble baths, and was said to have inspired the bombshell persona of another blond, Marilyn Monroe.

Saul Steinberg, 84, artist and cartoonist. The Romanian-born Jew studied architecture in Milan before arriving in Miami in 1942. A permanent outsider, he drew America as a schematized, imaginative and compelling nation of flat horizons broken by buttes or movie palaces, bulbous baroque autos, all-leg girls and cowboys teetering on high heels—erasing the distinction between cartoonist and "fine" artist.

Susan Strasberg, 60, actress. The daughter of acting teacher Lee Strasberg, she debuted on Broadway in 1955 as Anne Frank and appeared in such films as *Stage Struck* and *Picnic.*

Elizabeth (Liz) Tilberis, 51, editor of *Harper's Bazaar.* After rising from intern to editor in chief of British *Vogue*, the

Mel Torme

Manchester-born Tilberis took the helm at *Bazaar* in 1992 and quickly turned the sluggish magazine into an important arbiter of style. Known for her grace and decency, she campaigned for cancer awareness in the pages of *Bazaar* and in a 1998 memoir, *No Time to Die.*

Mel Torme, 73, consummate vocalist known, to his dismay, as the Velvet Fog. The son of Russian Jewish immigrants, Torme began performing at age 4; his voice's preternatural lushness was due in part to a small second growth of tonsil after a tonsillectomy. His artistry, however, was earned, and appreciated by fans from '40s bobby-soxers to '90s alternative rockers. Torme played several instruments and was an arranger and composer who wrote some 300 tunes, including (with Robert Wells) the hit *The Christmas Song.*

Franjo Tudjman, 77, President of Croatia. Though he was credited with gaining his country's independence from Yugoslavia in 1991, his nationalist policies fueled wars with Bosnian Muslims and Yugoslav Serbs.

Señor Wences (Wenceslao Moreno), 103, ventriloquist who created impish dummies out of his bare hand and a tiny wig. As a schoolboy in Spain, Moreno began using his hand as a puppet to amuse himself in school. On TV's '50s and '60s variety shows, he delighted audiences with sweetly silly exchanges between the hand puppet Johnny and cranky,

disembodied head-in-a-box Pedro: "All right?" "S'all right."

Morris West, 83, novelist whose characters struggled with faith and outlandish plots. Critics were unimpressed with his books—*The Devil's Advocate* and *The Shoes of the Fisherman* among them—but West sold 60 million of them worldwide.

William H. Whyte, 81, optimistic social thinker and urban planner. Whyte's opus on corporate America, *The Organization Man* (1956), warned against conformity and spiritlessness. After leaving his longtime post as an editor of FORTUNE, Whyte studied how humans and cities could best complement each other and helped inspire the makeover of New York City's Bryant Park.

Joe Williams, 80, jazz icon who sang with the Count Basie Orchestra. During his five-decade career, Williams, who in the '80s appeared on *The Cosby Show* as Grandpa Al, was known for perfect musical timing and the intimacy he conveyed in his blues and ballads, most famously his trademark *Every Day (I Have the Blues).*

Mario Zacchini, 87, "human cannonball" who performed for decades in the circus. The last of a family troupe of cannonballs, Zacchini claimed the toughest part about being ejected from a long barrel at 90 m.p.h. wasn't so much in the flying as in the landing in the net.

Señor Wences